FACTORS INFLUENCE HUMAN FAILURE DEVELOPMENT

JOHN LOK

Contents

PREFACE

Introduction

Human needs to concern what factors will influence us to develop success. I shall research different aspects how to influence human history development. Such as training , education, economy , medical etc. different aspects of capacity development. However, I hope this book can give a convincing and enticing initiation into an area of development knowledge and practice that is at the heart of what makes human development results sustainable over time. In the face of the current economic, climate and food crises, developing state and societal capacities to implement strategies that minimize the impact posed by these crises will remain critical for human existence towards achieving development objectives.

Nowadays, our societies are changing, any developed countries must need to continue to improve in order to avoid technology recession. In my this book, I shall explain why Japan will need to improve technology development , America will need to improve culture, England will need to improve education and India will need to improve medical technology.

I shall explain what reasons cause above these countries will need to improve as well as what negative economic influence will occur if these countries can not improve on above aspects. In macro economic view, what will be negative influences, if these countries can not improve these main aspects in future within 10 years. Readers can have more clear understanding why these developed countries need to continue improve in order to avoid recession occurrence. It is suitable to any readers who have interesting to pursue what factors will influence future human development, human will need to achieve success absolutely.

Prologue

contents
Chapter 1 Capacity training development Factor

Socio-economic and political environment factors influence huma development success

Strategy solves poverty on child education development

Influence of macro-environment factors p.5-26
Why do multi-organizations encounter cross-cultural communication challenges usually?

What factors influence the academic success to high school student learning development
What external factors impact of education quality on development goals to students.
Chapter 2
Daily life mind management training method

How mind management method
influences efficiency p.27-36

Raising Learning Ability Methods p.37-45

Intelligence methods raise
learning and remembering abilities p.46-54

Mind management methods to raise
employee productive efficiency p.55-63

THE RELATIONSHIP BEHAVIORAL
MIND AND RAISING ANALYTICAL
AND LEARNING ABILITY p.64-70

I

Capacity training development factor

What exactly are we meant by capacity development? In individual training development view point, for example, capacity about training development can be any effort to teach someone to do something , or to it better. For others, it may be about creating new institutions or strengthening old ones. Some see capacity development is a focus on education and training, when others view it as improving individual rights, access or freedom.

Thus, capacity development contains elements of all of the above. However, in organization training development view point, it sees capacity development as the progress through which individuals, organizations and societies obtain strengthen and maintain the capacities to set and achieve its own development objectives over time.

I shall indicate this interesting question: Based on your own personal experiences, have you ever wondered why certain government institutions perform better than others? I feel the reason is because capacity development is about transformations that empower individuals, leaders, organizations and societies. If something doesn't lead to change that is generated, guided and lead sustained by those whom it is meant to benefit than it can't be said to have enhanced capacity, even of it has served a valid development purpose. Then, the government institution will perform better or worse than others.

The difference between conventional training traditional development and capacity training development . I shall indicate the past conventional human development how for change in capacity human development. Firstly, on conventional training development aspect, it is the nowadays relationship between trainer and trainee(s). In general, any organization trainer will provide training to teach whose trainee(s) how to use the latest technology available on the market. Otherwise, on capacity training development aspect, training will be as an integral part of a comprehensive program addressing capacity issues on how to use the most reading available technology best suited to the organizations goals in a personal development plan, with build in incentive to apply the new skills, empowering / enabling trainee(s) to train others in using the technology , clearly articulating the benefits to personal performance to team performance and overall organizational efficiency and ability to fulfill its technology development.

Thus, the difference between traditional training development and capacity training development is that capacity training development can teach more new skills and competences developed responding to specific (individual and organizational) needs, incentives to apply the newly acquired skills and improve workplace performance, learning strategic to address future training needs, personal development recognized as a necessary means to improve organizational effectively performance. In short term, thus, it seems capacity training development can include these methods , such as a foreign expert hired to work to perform training needed functions (gap filling), or a project team provided training service housed within an organization. Those methods are one kind of outsourced training service to method to differ to common or general in-housing training department service method to provide training to any organization's employees.

Socio-economic and political environment factors influence
human development success

Development practitioners are increasingly aware of the role that social and political structurers play in shaping countries development paths and results. Failure to anticipate political and challenges is a chief cause of unsuccessful policy reform processes. So, by strengthening their capacity in the area of macro social and political analysis, human needs to understand what the conditions necessary for successful policy and successful implementation of pro-poor reforms, how to improve poor people life situation .
Hence, governments need to concern emphasis on the analysis of livelihoods and economic opportunities and their relationship to equity and social situation to different social groups within the different approaches to macro social and political analysis, there is a significant degree of variation across individual country cases.
Macro social and political analysis can focus on five main areas. The first is the inequities in society and obstacles

to it. The second concerns the risks to the livelihoods or human security of poor and social groups. The thirds area covers the political environment and relevant factors that contribute to the stability of the political system and the mobilization of coalitions for pro-poor perform. The fourth area is the space for collective action by citizen and the enabling environment for civil society. Finally, it focuses on the capacity of institutions to deliver basic products and services. I feel that the main shortcoming of macro social and political analysis itself, but rather the difficulty of translating its findings into actionable policy recommendations.

Finally , I shall recommend how to implement policy on the macro level to society. First, recommendation should address specific actions for removing barriers to social, such as lack of access to assets, employment opportunities and participation in policy making. Second, the analysis should lead to proposals on how on mitigate social and political risks, including conflict risks and risks deriving from planned development interventions. Consequently, macro social and political analysis should provide entry points for building coalitions for pro-poor change and managing policy reform processes (which include identifying political economy risks and social impacts of policy reforms).

In some cases, sector-specific poverty and social impact analysis may be integrated into the country-level analysis. In other cases, this may go beyond the scope of one particular study and additional analysis (such as a poverty and social impact analysis) may be recommended for a particular sector.

Strategy solves poverty on child education development

Poverty will affect a child's psychological and physical life development an education outcomes of life both directly and indirectly. However, nowadays, school readiness, or the child's ability to use and profit from school, has been recognized as playing a unique role in escape from poverty . Thus, it is a critical element, but needs to be supported by many other components of a poverty strategy, such as of improved opportunity structures and empowerment of families. Thus, I ensure poverty will affect child growth development and educational outcomes.

It brings this question: How to improve child growth development and educational outcomes for families in poverty? I shall recommend policy how to solve to improve child development and education for future research, programs and policies to reduce the negative consequences of poverty.

What does poverty mean? The first is whether poverty should be defined in economic terms, or should be defined in economic terms, or as part of a social disadvantage. The economic definition of poverty is typically based on income measures, will the absolute poverty line calculated as the food expenditure necessary to meet dietary needs. However, poor means lacking not only material assets and health , but also respecting on capabilities, such as social belonging, cultural identity aspects.

Thus, these factors which prevent groups on categories of people from moving out of poverty. Experiences of including material and want of food, housing and shelters, live. The analytic model experiences of ill-being including material lack and want of food, housing and shelter, livelihood, assets and money., hunger , pair and discomfort and poverty of time.

I feel the explanation mobility out of poverty , consists of interaction between two sets of factors : The first factor is that changes in the opportunity structure, consisting of the dominant institutional climate and social structures within which disadvantages to work to advance their interests and the second factor is that changes in the capabilities of poor individuals or groups to take purposeful actions,.

Child development refers to the interdependent social emotional functioning, which depend on the child's physical well-being, the family context and the larger social network. Educational outcomes include school readiness, educational achievements and years of schooling completed. School readiness means to skills children need to profit from the educational experiences of formal schooling. It is skills that affect children's ability to learn in school.

However, I feel seasons cause children raised in poverty, the major reason is become who are less in school. Thus, it seems that persuading to child independence readiness will have chances to solve poverty on child education development challenges. Collusion improving school readiness and children's development will reduce poverty related society. I feel to improve children's school readiness or family support for schooling is one good method to solve these challenges.

These include family based-safety, preschool programs, preschool interventions, programs to improve, programs to family-based safety, net program, preschool interventions, programs to improve parent's ability to support early learning and prove parent's ability to support early learning and comprehensive programs that improve children's development prior to school entry.

Influence of macro-environment factors

Influence of macro-environmental factors to the process of a foreign business development. Nowadays, in business development sector, multinational companies who prefer to establish welfare allowance to assist to foreign countries or international markets. However, I believe macro-economic factors as well as intercultural challenges will influence foreign-business development. The intercultural challenges will be considered the major human communication challenges to influence any foreign organizations' cooperation between domestic and overseas staffs.

The foreign businesses include automation industry, the electronic industry, the communications industry, the clothing industry, food industry or even the pharmacy industry etc. These businesses models often really are globalized or at least multi-national. However, they need employ many foreign workers / staffs to co-operate with the organization's domestic staffs/workers. Thus, they need to co-operate to finish every job duties or projects efficiently and effectively . It brings communication is very important to influence every worker's efficiency and performance and effort. If they have intercultural challenges, then it will cause every team member can not perform perfectly. Finally, the multi-national organizations will encounter fail if these foreign and domestic staffs/workers whose intercultural communications are not easily. Thus, multi-organization staffs/workers communication issue is valuable to be considered to any multi-organizations nowadays.

Moreover, micro as well as macro economic factors influence the economic activities of such complex company networks , when the multi-organization is either expanded of increased foreign or domestic staffs/workers numbers.

Thus, the complex company networks factors can be seen from the internal view point of a company, defined as the called micro-economic factors (Mussning, 2007).

Consequently, It will increase the foreign/domestic staffs or workers communication need when the multi-organization becomes complex. Thus, their cross-cultural differences become of critical importance for the success of multi-national business activities (Adler, 2008).

Why do multi-organizations encounter cross-cultural communication challenges usually?

To explain this situation, such as Haas (2006) explained that these stages for any one multi-organization expansion process: The first stage is the founding or functions to run a company are done by one single site. The second stage describes the increase of domestic market penetration to strengthen the market position. The aim of this stage is during expansion is the densification of the national market and establishing external sales agents in external markets. Not includes one the protected markets, sue to the higher entry barriers and therefore higher risks. The three stage deals with the aim in establishing own sales offices and subsidiaries in foreign markets to increase the market domination. In the final stage , during the expansion process stage, entering the protected markets with entry barriers and ongoing market densifications of already entered markets is the expansion model.

Thus, it seems cross cultural difference will have probability of influence to the efficiency of the integration to the origin organization. The cross-cultural differences include the power distance, uncertainty avoidance, individualism versus collectivism, and long-term versus short-term oriented persons as well as it will influence the efficiency of the integration process , it can be measured with their characteristics, such as time, cost, duration, customer retention and effort.

Consequently, doing business with a subsidiary in a foreign country always has to do with cross cultural management. Every single individual person has to think about the differences in term of culture and to consider about the cultures consists three parts of basic differences: human relationships, the feeling and interpreting of time and the attitude to the environment (Trompenaars, 1994).

What factors influence the academic success to high school student

learning development

Why do students feel difficulty to learn in whose growth stage? Do these environment factors influence whose learning effort? Do these something wrong learning attitude to influence whose learning effort? Do they lack to arrange the timetable discipline to learn?

However, I feel there are student personal development in growth stage challenges are more than the environment factors to influence who succeed to learning. It means that their learning behavior factor will be the major factor to influence whose learning effort.

I shall focus on answer to this learning success question regarding the learning behavior of the student himself/ herself. My hypothesis is that any student must attempt to arrange have something to do with whose success in school, even the foolish student who must have something to do with whose success in school also.

I want to find out of these were social or family conditions, other previous experiences (e.g. schooling) environment factors or the student personal attributes that might explain why some succeed and some do not.

In fact, student feel difficult to learn, the personal factors can include mental health problems, e.g. suicidal behavior, such as absence due to illness; antisocial acts as measured by inappropriate , and rebellious behavior in an out of class as well as school-related problems, such as measured by academic failure. Thus, these causes will be the student personal behavior factors to influence whose learning effort were more serious than the environment factors. Thus, if the student had health body and right attitude. Then who will have positive learning motivation effort. Otherwise, if the student had poor and wrong learning attitude, then who will have negative learning effort.

Brofenbrenner as cited in Benard,(1991) referred to an increasing acceptance in the child development field of the transactional ecological model of human development. This model views the human personality as a self righting mechanism that is engaged in active ongoing adaptation to its environment. Thus, although the learning environment is poor, e.g. the student's family is poor or his /her house is not clean and small , these factors won't influence whose learning effort. If the student could have a positive learning behavior. The, he/she can be active ongoing adaptation to easily fight its poor learning environment.

Thus, I believe that poor learning environment won't be the major factor to influence the student personal learning effort. The student himself/herself learning behavior and attitude will be the major factor to influence the student personal learning effort. Nowadays, education professionals ought need to considered how to train teachers' whose students to develop their learning effort to raise their confidence to fright any poor environment factor influence to their further learning career in any schooling stages.

What external factors impact of education quality on development goals to students.

I feel how to distribution of personal incomes in society which is strongly related to the amount of education people have had. Because , generally speaking more schooling means higher lifetime incomes for students working life. These outcomes are long term . It is not people's income when in their first job, but their income other their working life. Thus, any noticeable effects of the current quality of schooling on the distribution of skills and income will become apparent some years in the future, when those now in school become a significant part of the labor force. I also feel future general improvements in productivity throughout the economy are likely to lead to larger returns to higher skill levels.

Obviously, students who do better in school, as evidenced by either examination grades or scores on standardized achievement tests, tend to go further in school or university. By the same way, the intangible costs of improvements in school quality if reflected in increased attainment by learners, are less than who appear, perhaps substantially because of the resulting reductions in rates of learning repetition if the education quality is improved to be taught to every student to reduce their time to be spent to study the same course more than one year repetition. Thus, higher student achievement keeps students in school longer, which leads, rates at all levels of schooling . According in countries where schools are dysfunctional and grade repetition is high. Some improvements in quality may be largely self-financing by reducing the average time completers spend in school. Thus, how to raise the education quality will be important issue to raise very student's learning ability and to shorten every one learning time to complete whose courses in school.

Clearly, differences in education quality can affect human behavior in ways that facilitate the achievement of a wide range of human goals. It brings this question: How to measure education quality? I feel that tests of cognitive achievement are in complete proxies for the measurement of the quality of education. They tell nothing about values, capacities or other non-cognitive skills that are important aims of education. Moreover, if the extent of value added by schooling , even in the cognitive domain, is to be known, such tests need to be supplemented by measures of the background characteristics that learners bring to formal education. However , I feel that it is possible to compare learning achievement scores among the countries within each study, but nor among the studies themselves that the method is good measurement of the education quality.

When we know how to compare learning achievement scores among the countries within each study to measure this method is good measurement of education quality. Then , it brings this question: What factors influence education quality? It feel that some aspects of how the school environments appear to have improved over the period, it can influence the school education quality to be provided to its students. For example, education facilities , which can influence the students feel learning easily or difficult. If the school can provide comfortable , kindly , friendly sympathy learning environment and enough education facilities to provide to its students to study. Then, I believe it will provide good quality of education to let its students to learn.

Moreover, enough education facilities supply can influence every teacher's teaching effort. Consequently, I believe education facilities can influence education environment as well as education environment can influence education quality to improve every student learning effort importantly.

In conclusion, I feel the environment factors can influence student behavioral differences. The reasons are because every student needs to change whose learning attitude to adapt variable learning environment influence factors. For example, some students need to change their leisure time to adapt learning time, due to their school learning timetable is often changed. It will influence their studying effort indirectly. Thus, I believe personal learning behavior factor and environment changing factors will influence the academic success to high school student learning development in their studying career importantly.

Reference

Adler, Nancy J., Gunderson, Allison, (2008); International dimensions of organizational behavior, 5th edition, Mascon: Thomson higher education, p.12

Benard, B. (1991). Fostering resillency in kids: Protective factors in the family , school and community, Portland, OR: Northwest regional educational laboratory

Hass, Stans-Dieter; Neumair, Siman Martin; (2006): International Mirtschatt: Rahmenbedingungen, Akteure, Raumliche Prozesse; 1st edition; Munich: Oldenbourg Wissenschaftsverlag., p. 692

Mussning, Wener, (2007), Strategien entwickeln and umsetzen; 1st edition, Wien: Linde Verlag., p.41

Trompenarrs, Fons: (1994); Handbuch Global Management, 1st edition Wienetal: Econ Verlag, p.21

II

Daily life mind management training method

"What is the single most important skill you can learn to increase your happiness and success? I believe that training your mind will be the only important methods. Training your mind can be trained to keep health physical activities, then when you have health physical activities,e.g. keeping good life habit, then you will raise mind energy to raise learning ability or working efficiency more easier. These methods can include as below:

· How many thoughts you have in a day, you need to attempt to calculate, because if you discovered that you have too much rubblish mind to influence you need to spend extra time to decide any important matters every day. Then, you will lose time and nervous to do any important matters every day.

Why sports people need mind management? If sports people have good mind managment, then they can concentrate enough nervous to learn how to raise their sports ability to win any sport competition more easily.

How thoughts have energy to achieve learning or/and working efficiencies to be raised? Because if one student has good mind, then he/she can spend enough time to learn and he/she won't spend time to learn rubblish matters as well as if one working person has good min, then he/she can spend enough time to concentrate nervous to do his/her work more efficiently.

How you are not thoughts, then you will have much chance to lose your efficiency to work when you are one working person or waste your nervous to learn rubblish knowledge when you are one student.

How mind management needs training because you can improve your learning ability to raise your working efficiency or raise your nervous to learn.

How Mind management can improve your personal and professional life because mind management is only the best method to help students to raise leaning ability in schools as well as working people to raise working efficiencies in offices.

I shall explain that why daily life mind management learning method will be one good raising learning ability and working efficiency method as below:

Everyone is familiar with all-out energy drain -- that exhausted day (or night) when no matter how to spend extra time to choose to watch that new movie, choose to buy which brand of fabulous shoe sale, or find whose friends to meet friendly barbecue together etc. less important lesisure activities,

What the student or the working person can be harder to recognize is a low-grade energy drain. In this case, he/she may not necessarily feel the classic signs of exhaustion -- like achy muscles or that all-over tired feeling. What the student or the working person does experience is an increasing lack of get-up-and-go for many of the activities that the learner or the working person used to love.

I shall suggest some physical activities to raise mind management energy method as below:

(1) Keeping health diet

Eating a balanced diet can help ensure your vitamin and mineral needs are met. But if you still find yourself eat much rubblish food, you could have a slight magnesium deficiency.

Some health diet professionals indicate that "This mineral is needed for more than 300 biochemical reactions in the body, including breaking down glucose into energy," They says. "So when levels are even a little low, energy can drop."

In a study done at the Department of Agriculture's Human Nutrition Research Center in Grand Forks, N.D., women with magnesium deficiencies had higher heart rates and required more oxygen to do physical tasks than they did after their magnesium levels were restored. In essence, their bodies were working harder which, over time. They also recommended daily intake of magnesium is around 300 milligrams for women and 350 milligrams for men. To make sure you're getting enough, they suggests:

· Add a handful of almonds, hazelnuts or cashews to your daily diet.

· Increase your intake of whole grains, particularly bran cereal.

· Eat more fish, especially halibut.

So, health diet professionals believe that it has close relationship to influence student learning ability and working person work efficiency between health diet and physical mind management skill.

(2) Walk Around the Block

While it may seem as if moving about when you feel exhausted is the quickest route to feeling more exhausted, the opposite is true. Experts say that increasing physical activity -- particularly walking -- increases energy. Then, walking life habit will raise your learning ability and improving working efficiencies effectively.

"I like walking because it's accessible, easy to do, doesn't need training or equipment and you can do it anywhere," says Rita Redberg, MD, science advisor to the American Heart Association's "Choose To Move" program. In experiments conducted by Robert Thayer, PhD, at California State University, a brisk 10-minute walk not only increased energy, but the effects lasted up to two hours. And when the daily 10-minute walks continued for three weeks, overall energy levels and mood were lifted. So, spending some extra time life day walking activity , it can raise your nervous to learn anythings or improve efficiency to do anythings more effectively. Time management to do walking activities daily , it can help any students and working people to concentrate on doing any tasks or learning any new knowledge more easily.

(3) Take a Power Nap

Research has shown that both information overload and pushing our brains too hard can zap energy. But studies by the National Institutes of Mental Health found that a 60-minute "power nap" can not only
reverse the mind-numbing effects of information overload, it may also help us to better retain what we have learned.

So, we ought need have suitable time to nap in order to raise our learning ability more effectively every day.

(4) Reduce Stress and Deal With Anger

One of the biggest energy zappers is stress, says psychologist Paul Baard, PhD.

"Stress is the result of anxiety, and anxiety uses up a whole lot of our energy," says Baard, a sports psychologist at Fordham University in the Bronx, N.Y.Like worry or fear, Baard says, stress can leave you mentally and physically exhausted -- even if you've spent the day in bed. More commonly, he says, low but chronic levels of stress erode energy levels,

so over time you find yourself doing less and feeling it more.

In much the same way, unexpressed anger can give a one-two punch to your energy level. The reason: "We're expending all our energy trying to contain our angry feelings, and that can be exhausting," Baard tells WebMD.

The good news, says Baard, is that we can counter these energy killers by programming more relaxation activities into our day. While for many folks, increasing exercise burns off the chemical effects of stress and anger, others find relief in quiet pursuits: listening to music, reading a steamy romance novel, or even just talking on the phone."Whatever is relaxing for you will reduce tension and that will help increase energy," Hence, sometime to spend time to listen music or read books or watch movies, these entertainment activities can help me to reduce stress or workload effectively.

(5) Drink More Water and Less Alcohol

You may already know that it's easy to confuse signals of hunger with thirst (we think we need food when we really need water).

But did you know that thirst can also masquerade as fatigue?The solution is simple: a tall, cool glass of water. This is particularly important to boost energy after exercise,
when your body is likely to be craving fluids, Ayoob says.

Conversely, if you find yourself frequently
fatigued even after a good night's sleep, try cutting down on alcohol during the evening hours. 'While alcohol initially helps you fall asleep, it also interferes with deep sleep, so you're not getting the rest By cutting down on alcohol before bedtime, you'll get a better night's rest, which is bound to result in more energy the next day.

Eat More Whole Grains and Less Sugar .The key here is keeping blood sugar balanced so energy is constant."When you're eating a sweet food, you get a spike in blood sugar, which gives you an initial burst of energy," "But that's followed by a rapid drop in blood sugar, which in turn can leave you feeling very wiped out. Do that enough times a day, and by evening you're feeling exhausted.
"But, if you eat a lot of whole grains, which provide a slow and steady release of fuel,
your energy will be consistent and balanced, so by day's end you'll feel less tired.Hence, drinking much water and drinking less alcohol , this diet activity will influence students' learning ability and working people working efficiency effectively.

(6) Power snacking is more than just eating between meal. So, a treat that combines protein, a little fat and some fiber
--
like peanut butter on a whole-wheat cracker, or some yogurt with a handful of nuts.
"The carbs offer a quick pick-me-up, the protein keeps your

energy up, and the fat makes the energy last. So, we needs to eat more foods , they have high protein, because high protein foods can raise my nervous and mind and analytic abilities to be raised effectively.

How mind management method
influences efficiency

Has it close relationship betwern being effective at work And essential traits and Skills and good mind management training method?

We need to answer these question before we investigate this answer . Are you as effective, efficient and productive as you could be?

Do you consider yourself to be effective at work? Although many of us like to think that we're 100 percent effective, the truth is that most of us have strengths and weaknesses that impact our effectiveness.

Many of us could benefit from tweaking at least a few of our skills, in order to become even more effective. For instance, perhaps you've always excelled at time management. But how much time do you put into learning new skills, or staying on top of industry trends?

Or, maybe you're adept at managing the considerable demands you face day-to-day. But, when things get really to let you feel difficulties, your communication skills start to suffer as stress levels begin to rise.

Being truly effective at work can pay off now and throughout our careers. Effective workers get exciting projects, win important clients, and are well respected by their colleagues and bosses. But how can you become more effective, and make sure that you don't miss out on these great opportunities? And what should you focus on?

We'll look at the skills you can develop in order to become more effective at work, and we'll review strategies and resources that you can use to increase your effectiveness.

Step 1: Identify Priorities

If someone asked you what your job was truly about, would you have a good answer?

One of the most crucial steps in becoming fully effective is to know your purpose at work. After all, if you don't know what your job is there to achieve, how can you set appropriate priorities? (If you don't set priorities, you'll be forever do any tasks efficiently and effectively and you are unable to tell the difference between what's important, and what isn't.)

To identify your job's true purpose and define what you need to achieve in your current position, perform a job analysis .

This step will help you uncover your most important objectives, so that you can start prioritizing tasks effectively.

Step 2: Adopt a Good Attitude

Effective workers have a "good attitude." But what does this really mean? People with a good attitude take the initiative whenever they can. They willingly help a colleague in need, they pick up the slack when someone is off sick, and they make sure that their work is done to the highest standards. "Good enough" is never quite good enough for them!

A good attitude at work will do more than just earn you respect: setting standards for your work and your behavior means that
you're taking responsibility for yourself. This admirable trait is hard to find in many organizations. But

demonstrating ethical
decision-making and integrity could open many doors for you in the future. So, focus on adopting a good attitude at work, and make decisions that intuitively "ring true." At the very least, you'll sleep easier at night!

Step 3: Build Essential Skills

Chances are that you have a lot of competing demands on your time. One of the best ways of becoming more effective at
work is to learn how to manage your time more efficiently. Other key areas include learning how to manage stress, improving your communication skills, and taking action on career development. All of these can have a major impact on your effectiveness at work.

Step 4:Time Management/Productivity

Probably the most crucial thing that you can do to become more effective at work is to learn how to manage your time.
Without this skill, your days will feel like a frantic race, with every project, email, and phone call competing for your attention.
Start by looking at your daily schedule. Do you know how you spend your time every day? If not, the answer might surprise
you! Use an Activity Log to analyze how much time you're devoting to your various tasks, like meetings, checking email, and making phone calls. It can be an eye-opening experience to look at this objectively, especially if you discover that you're spending lots of time on tasks that don't help you meet your objectives.

Once you know how much time you're devoting to different tasks, you need to learn how to prioritize them. If you know which

jobs are important, and which can be rescheduled or delegated, you'll be able to focus on the work that brings the most value.

To keep track of it all, use an organizing tool like a To-Do List or (better still) an Action Program , to make sure you don't forget vital tasks and commitments.

Being effective at work means you use time to your advantage. Schedule your highest value work for the times of day when you're

feeling the most energetic. This increases the likelihood that you'll resist distractions and enter a state of flow when working.

For example, is This a Morning Task? , helps you identify your peak energy time, so that you can schedule work accordingly; and our Are you a Procrastinator? self-test will help you deal with a serious, effectiveness-killing habit.

Step 5:Setting Goal

Goal setting is another important element in working productively. Once you've done a Job Analysis , you should have a clear

sense of what your role is all about. Use this information to set short and long-term goals. The advantage of doing this is that

your goals act as a roadmap – after all, you'll never get anywhere if you don't know where you're going! Good organization is also important for working effectively and productively. If you're disorganized, you can waste a huge amount of time just looking for lost items. So learn how to file properly, and find out how to create an effective schedule .

Step 6: Effective Communication Skills

Think about just how often we communicate every day. We make phone calls, attend meetings, write emails, give presentations, talk to customers, and so on. We can seem to spend all day communicating with the people around us. This is why good communication skills are essential, especially when your goal is to work more effectively.

Step 6 :Start by developing your active listening skills.

This means that you're making a concerted effort to really hear and understand
what other people are saying to you.Don't let yourself become distracted by what's going on around you, and don't plan out what you're going to say next,while the other person is talking. Instead, just listen to what they're saying. You may well be surprised at how much miscommunication can be avoided simply by listening actively.

Step 7: look at your writing skills .

How well do you communicate in writing? Start with your emails. Most of us write dozens of emails every day. But there are many techniques that we can use to make sure we write effective emails – ones that actually get read!For instance, always keep to one main topic when writing an email.

Putting several important topics in one message will make it difficult for your colleague to prioritize and sort the information. If you do need to bring up several different points, then number them sequentially, or split them into separate messages, with relevant subject headings.

Of course, we do a lot more writing than just email. We write through IM , we write reports , and we create presentations .
You'll be more effective in your role if you learn how to communicate better across all these media, and your boss and colleagues are bound to appreciate your skills, since they'll be the main beneficiaries!

Step 8: Finding Stress Source and solutions
A little bit of pressure can be a good thing. But when pressure exceeds your ability to cope with it effectively, your productivity goes down, and your mood suffers. You also lose your ability to make solid, rational decisions;
and excessive stress can cause health problems, both in the short and long term.
No matter what you do, you'll likely experience stress numerous times throughout your career, perhaps even on a regular basis.
This is why learning how to manage stress is a key factor in becoming more effective at work.
Try to get a good night's sleep every night, and do your best to avoid taking work home with you. It's also important to
relax when you get home in the evening.
If you're not sure what triggers your stress, keep a stress diary for a week or two. This helps you to identify the events that cause you stress, and understand the degree to which you experience it. When you're feeling calm,
you can then analyze these triggers and come up with effective strategies for managing them.

Step 9: Career Development/Learning

No matter what your field is, it's important that you keep learning and developing your skills.To begin with, carry out a Personal SWOT Analysis to identify the areas that you need to work on. In addition to the technical skills required to do your job, you also need to focus on soft skills .

These include areas such as leadership skills, problem solving techniques, emotional intelligence skills , and creative thinking . Anything you can do to enhance these skills will pay off in the workplace. Also, consider if there are any qualifications that you don't have that a reasonable person would consider

appropriate for your field. If so, could this be holding you back from an advancement or promotion? For instance, would it be useful to have a particular degree or other certification if you want to apply for a management position? Are you lacking any specific skills? In some roles, keeping up-to-date with developments in your industry helps you stay relevant. It will

help you do your job better, especially as you climb the ranks.

III

Raising Learning Ability Methods

Cognitive strategies are useful tools in assisting students with learning problems. The term "cognitive strategies" in its simplest form is the use of the mind (cognition) to solve a problem or complete a task. Cognitive strategies provide a structure for learning when a task cannot be completed through a series of steps. For example, algorithms in mathematics provide a series of steps to solve a problem. Attention to the steps results in successful completion of the problem. In contrast, reading comprehension, a complex task, is a good example of a task that does not follow a series of steps. Further explanation is provided below.

A cognitive strategy serves to support the learner as he or she develops internal procedures that enable him/her to perform tasks that are complex (Rosenshine, 1997). Reading comprehension is an area where cognitive strategies are important. A self-questioning strategy can help students understand what they read. Rosenshine states that the act of creating

questions does not lead directly to comprehension. Instead, students search the text and combine information as they generate

questions; then they comprehend what they have read.

The use of cognitive strategies can increase the efficiency with which the learner approaches a learning task. These academic

tasks can include, but are not limited to, remembering and applying information from course content, constructing sentences and paragraphs, editing written work, paraphrasing, and classifying information to be learned.

In a classroom where cognitive strategies are used, the teacher fulfills a pivotal role, bridging the gap between student and content/skill to be learned. This role requires an understanding of the task to be completed, as well as knowledge of an approach (or approaches) to the task that he/she can communicate to the learner.

Content Enhancement first step ?

Impacting both the task and the learner using cognitive strategies is referred to as Content Enhancement.

1. Teachers evaluate the content they cover.

2. Teachers determine the necessary approaches to learning for student success.

3. Teachers teach with routines and instructional supports that assist students as they apply appropriate techniques and strategies.

In this way, the teacher emphasizes what the students should learn, or the "product" of learning. In addition, the teacher models the how or "process" of learning. The teaching steps may include as below:

Content Evaluation second step?

When a teacher is comfortable with the content he/she is teaching, he/she knows which parts are the most important, the most interesting and the easiest (or hardest) to learn. The teacher evaluates the content with various questions in mind:

How important is this information to my students?

Is any of this information irrelevant to the point I can minimize or exclude it?

How will my students use this information beyond my classroom (in general education classrooms, college and/or career settings, etc.) ?

What parts of this information do I think my students will grasp quickly?

What parts of this information do I think my students will need "extras" (more time, more examples, peer help, more explanation,

applications, etc.) ?

How should I pace the presentation?

Which evaluations are going to help me know that my students understand this information?

The more experienced the teacher is with content, the better he/she will be able to plan students' cognitive journey through the information or skills that will be unfamiliar to them.

Determination of necessary approaches

third step

Now the teacher's attention turns to his/her knowledge of the students. Student characteristics such as intellectual ability, interest in the subject, and general motivation to learn are considered. The teacher selects learning approaches that complement the learner characteristics while ensuring success with the content.

A teacher who teaches cognitive strategies well will connect learner and task. A strategy will be chosen because it is the best strategy for BOTH the learner's characteristics and the task and/or content that needs to be mastered.

Routines and instructional supports fourth step

Once the best strategy or strategies have been selected, the teacher begins the work of teaching the strategy to the student(s). Explicit instruction is used to impart the components or steps of the strategy. Often the strategy will include actions or routines that are repeated each time the strategy is implemented. Additional instructional supports such as guided practice, independent practice, verbal practice, and written or oral tests may also be used.

I shall indiate A Real-Life Example to explain how above methods can help students to raise learning abilities as below:

You can compare the teaching of cognitive strategies to teaching a friend to drive in your hometown. Because you are in your hometown, you know the area, or content, very well. In addition, the person you are teaching to drive is your friend, so you also know the learner well. This knowledge can make your teaching more efficient, because you have two areas of expertise (the content and the learner) at your disposal. You will use a combination of explicit instructions (turn left on Church Street) and supports maps, the rule that "all avenues run North-South") to teach your friend how to navigate around town.

You may also use verbal directions as opposed to maps, depending on your friend's preferred mode of information. Just as important, you can avoid situations that could become barriers to learning (and your friendship). For example, if your friend tends to be anxious, you will NOT begin your instruction during rush hour!

How to Select Cognitive Strategies methods to teach your students?

Because they are diverse and highly relevant to tasks, the use of cognitive strategies by teachers and students can significantly impact important learning outcomes for students. I shall suggest some

Cognitive Strategies for Special Connections as below:

Strategy Type

(1) Orienting Strategies

Student's attention is drawn to a task through teacher input, highlighted material, and/or student self-regulation.

(2) Teacher cue to "listen carefully"Boldface type of Specific Aids for Attention

Student's attention is maintained by connecting a concrete object or other cue to the task. A special pencil cues the student to pay special attention to punctuation when he is writing sentences.

(3) Specific Aids for Problem-Solving or Memorization

Student's problem-solving is enhanced by connecting a concrete object or other cue to the task. Concrete objects are used in solving math problems.

(4) Rehearsal

Student practices (rehearses) target information through verbalization, visual study, or other means. Students practice vocabulary and definitions through games where they must orally repeat target information.

(5) Elaboration

Student expands target information by relating other information to it (ex. creating a phrase, making an analogy). Students relate the life of an ant colony to their community.

(6) Transformation

Student simplifies target information by converting difficult or unfamiliar information into more manageable information.

Procedures for protecting oneself from being burned are learned as "Stop, Drop, and Roll".

(7) Imagery*

Student transforms target information by creating meaningful visual, auditory, or kinesthetic images of the information.

Visualization of a scene described in a passage

(8) Mnemonics*

Student transforms target information by relating a cue word, phrase, or sentence to the target information.

(9) Organization

Student categorizes, sequences or otherwise organizes information for more efficient recall and use. Words in lists are placed in categories. *Imagery and Mnemonics can be considered special types of transformational strategies.

In conclusion, the use of cognitive strategies can increase the efficiency and confidence with which the learner approaches a learning task, as well as his/her ability to develop a product, retain essential information, or perform a skill. While teaching cognitive strategies requires a high degree of commitment from both the teacher and learner, the results are well worth the effort.

Intelligence methods raise
learning and remembering abilities

What is "Intelligence"? First of all, let me explain what I mean when I say the word "intelligence". To be clear, I'm not just talking about increasing the volume of facts or bits of

knowledge you can accumulate,
or what is referred to as crystallized intelligence—this isn't fluency or memorization training—it's almost the opposite, actually. I'm talking about increasing your fluid intelligence, or your capacity to learn new information, retain it, then use that new knowledge as a foundation to solve the next problem,
or learn the next new skill, and so on.

Now, while working memory is not synonymous with intelligence, working memory correlates with intelligence to a large degree. In order to generate successfully intelligent output, a good working memory is pretty important. So to make the most of your intelligence, improving your working memory will help this significantly—like using
the very best and latest parts to help a machine to perform at its peak.

Thus, Anyone can increase their cognitive ability, no matter what your starting point is.
The effect can be gained by training on tasks that don't resemble the test questions. How Can I Put This Research To Practical Use For My Own Benefit?

There is a reason why the dual n-back task was so successful at increasing cognitive ability. It involves dividing your attention between competing stimuli, multimodal in fashion (one visual, one auditory).
It requires you to focus on specific details while ignoring irrelevant information, which helps to improve your working memory over time, gradually increasing your ability to multi-task the information effectively.

In addition, the stimulus was constantly switched, so there was never a "training to the test questions" phenomenon—it was always different. If you've never taken the dual n-back test, let me tell you this: I'm not surprised there was so much cognitive gain from practicing this activity.

Eventually, you will run out of cards in the deck or sounds in the array (the experiment lasted between 2 weeks to 3 weeks), so it isn't practical to think that if you want to continually increase your brain power over the course of your lifetime, that the dual n-back alone will do the trick. Also, you'll get bored with it and stop doing it. I know I would. Not to mention the time it takes to train in this activity—we all have busy lives! So we need to think of how to simulate the same types of heavy-duty brain thrashing—using multimodal methods—that can be applied to your normal life, while still maintaining the maximum benefits, in order to get the cognitive growth.

So, taking all of this into account, I have come up with three primary elements involved in increasing your mind or brain intelligence, or cognitive ability. Like I said, it would be impractical to constantly practice the dual n-back task or variations thereof every day for the rest of your life to reap cognitive benefits. But it isn't impractical to adopt lifestyle changes that will have the same—and even greater cognitive benefits. These can be implemented every day, to get you the benefits of intense entire-brain training, and should transfer to gains in overall cognitive functioning as well.

These three primary principles are:

1. Think Creatively, e.g. finding any new knowledge that you feel that you had not mind before. Creating new synaptic connections with every new activity you engage in. These connections build on each other, increasing your neural

activity, creating more connections to build on other connections—learning is taking place. If you adopt these as fundamental guidelines, I guarantee you will be performing at your peak ability, surpassing even what you believe you are capable of—all without artificial enhancement. Best part: Science supports these principles by way of data! Teachers created not only innovative methods of creative teaching in the classroom, but generated assessment procedures that tested the students in ways that got them to think about the problems in creative and practical ways,

as well as analytical, instead of just memorizing facts.

2. Do Things The Hard Way, attempt to do any things that you feel difficulties and you ought not feel or fear failure because fail is the success in beginning. An area of interest in recent research is neural plasticity as a factor in individual differences in intelligence. Plasticity is referring to the number of connections made between neurons, how that affects subsequent connections, and how long-lasting those connections are. Basically, it means how much new information

you are able to take in, and if you are able to retain it, making lasting changes to your brain. Constantly exposing yourself to new things helps puts your brain in a primed state for learning, which not only kicks motivation

into high gear, but it stimulates neurogenesis—the creation of new neurons—and prepares your brain for learning.

There are absolutely oodles of terrible things written and promoted on how to "train your brain" to "get smarter". When I speak of "brain training games", I'm referring to the memorization and fluency-type games, intended to increase your speed of processing, etc, such as Sudoku, that they tell you to do in your "idle time" (complete oxymoron,

regarding increasing cognition). I'm going to shatter some of that stuff you've previously heard about brain training games. Here goes: They don't work. Individual brain training games don't make you smarter—they
make you more proficient at the brain training games.

Now, they do serve a purpose, but it is short-lived. The key to getting something out of those types of cognitive activities sort of relates to the first principle of seeking novelty. Once you master one of those cognitive
activities in the brain-training game, you need to move on to the next challenging activity. Now move along to the next type of challenging game. There is research that supports this logic.

A few years ago, scientist Richard Haier wanted to see if you could increase your cognitive ability by intensely training on novel mental activities for a period of several weeks. They used the video game Tetris as the novel
activity, and used people who had never played the game before as subjects (I know—can you believe they exist?!).

What they found, was that after training for several weeks on the game Tetris, the subjects experienced an increase
in cortical thickness, as well as an increase in cortical activity, as evidenced by the increase in how much glucose was used in that area of the brain. Basically, the brain used more energy during those training times, and bulked up in thickness—which means more neural connections, or new learned expertise—after this intense training. right? Here's the thing: After that initial explosion of cognitive growth, they noticed a decline in both cortical thickness, as well as the amount of glucose used during that task. The brain scans showed less brain activity during the game-playing, instead of more, as in the previous days.

Why the drop?

So, their brains got more efficient. Efficiency is not your friend when it comes to cognitive growth. In order to keep your brain making new connections and
keeping them active, you need to keep moving on to another challenging activity as soon as you reach the point of mastery
in the one you are engaging in. You want to be in a constant state of slight discomfort, struggling to barely achieve whatever it is you are trying to do.

I mentioned earlier that efficiency is not your friend if you are trying to increase your intelligence. Unfortunately, many things in life are centered on trying to make everything more efficient. This is so we can do more things, in a shorter amount of time, expending the least amount of physical and mental energy possible. However, this isn't doing your brain any favors.

Take one object of modern convenience, GPS. GPS is an amazing invention. I am one of those people GPS was invented for. My sense of direction is terrible. I get lost all the time. So when GPS came along, I was
thanking my lucky stars. But you know what? After using GPS for a short time, I found that my sense of direction was worse. If I failed to have it with me, I was even more lost than before.

Technology does a lot to make things in life easier, faster, more efficient, but sometimes our cognitive skills
can suffer as a result of these shortcuts, and hurt us in the long run. Now, before everyone starts screaming and emailing my transhumanist friends to say that I've sinned by trashing tech—that's not what I'm doing.

Look at it this way: Driving to work takes less physical energy, saves time, and it's probably more convenient and pleasant than walking. Not a big deal. But if you drove everywhere you went, or spent your life on a Segway, even to go very short distances, you aren't going to be expending any physical energy. Over time, your muscles will

atrophy, your physical state will weaken, and you'll probably gain weight. Your overall health will probably decline as a result.

Your brain needs exercise as well. If you stop using your problem-solving skills, your spatial skills, your logical skills, your cognitive skills—how do you expect your brain to stay in top shape—never mind improve? Think about modern conveniences that are helpful, but when relied on too much, can hurt your skill in that domain. Translation software: amazing, but my multilingual skills have declined since I started using it more.

There are times when using technology is warranted and necessary. But there are times when it's better to say no to shortcuts and use your brain, as long as you can afford the luxury of time and energy. Walking to work every so often or taking the stairs instead of the elevator a few times a week is recommended to

stay in good physical shape. Don't you want your brain to be fit as well? Lay off the GPS once in a while, and do your spatial and problem-solving skills a favor. Keep it handy, but try navigating naked first. Your brain will thank you.

3. Network, making more social network in you life, e.g. going to church, going to library , going to travelling, making frinds from internet etc. different network channel, because you can discuss any difficulties matters with other people when you need to argue as well as it can raise your analytical ability when you are arguing. So, you have much useful time to earn other people's different ideas or opinions when you need to solve any challenges every

day.

When you attempt to do above behaviors every day. consequently, it can brings this result , such as :Excellent learning condition = Novel Activity—>triggers dopamine—>creates a higher motivational state—>which fuels engagement and primes neurons—>neurogenesis can take place + increase in synaptic plasticity (increase in new neural

connections, or learning).

And that brings us to the last element to maximize your cognitive potential: Networking. What's great about this last objective is that if you are doing the other four things, you are probably already doing this as

well. If not, start. Immediately. By networking with other people—either through social media such as Facebook or Twitter, or in face-to-face

interactions—you are exposing yourself to the kinds of situations that are going to make objectives 1-2 much easier to achieve.

By exposing yourself to new people, ideas, and environments, you are opening yourself up to new opportunities for cognitive growth. Being in the presence of other people who may be outside of your immediate field gives you opportunities to see problems from a new perspective, or offer insight in ways that you had never thought of before. Learning is all about exposing yourself to new things and taking in that information in ways that are meaningful and unique—networking with other people is a great way to make that happen. I'm not even going to get into the social benefits and emotional well-being that is derived

from networking as a factor here, but that is just an added perk.

Mind management methods to raise employee productive efficiency

Employees are at their desks for an average of about five hours every day, and companies are paying for that time.

But often the results of an employee's work vs. time spent don't exactly match up. A model employee that seems perfectly productive can turn out to be one of the worst offenders.

Accordingly, I've compiled a list of steps to help improve efficiency, engagement and productivity in the workplace.

Some of them may seem to defy logic but entrepreneurs will find that following them can lead to a happier workplace and an increased ROI.

1. Relax on Internet restrictions.

Too often, employers overly restrict the use of the Internet. This may be out of fear

that company-owned computers might be misused. However, with the amount of resources available online,

the truth is that most tasks can be completed more efficiently if employees are allowed to roam freely online in ways not anticipated by the employer.

A perfect example is the growing use of social media, which often times has a legitimate business purpose. Marketing on social media is becoming increasingly important to help businesses and employees grow, and social media can be useful in keeping up to date with competitors' latest moves. There are many employers today who simply do not allow employees to use social platforms at work.It's not always about Facebook; people can have zero productivity without even opening it. On the other hand, some employees can be super-productive social networking gurus.

2. Consistently measure overall employee activity and productivity.

In a way, measuring productivity to increase ROI is similar to sales and marketing data. In order to increase number of leads, you have to start counting those leads. If you want to increase sales, understanding the source of current sales is imperative. Breaking an entire process of working with customers in to steps, measuring every step and experimenting with improvements can lead to an increase in ROI.

The same can be said about employee-performance management. To improve the structure in general, you have to see the entire picture -- it's even better if you can have a recorded history to compare. That way, managers can ask,"how are we doing in this May 2015 in comparison to May 2014 when we worked from different office?" Or "How many productive hours per day does the financial team have now, compared to last month when we had less on the payroll?"
In other words, in order to improve productivity stats, the reporting numbers must come first to get a clear idea what needs to be improved.

Recording usage of websites and applications can help companies keep track of productivity levels, as long as it's handled the right way. I've typically found that when employers are open about monitoring desktops, it creates a transparent, accountable environment. Managers shouldn't go into it with a lazy attitude but rather with the mindset to identify overall trends and find ways to improve productivity.

3. Set goals and use results to help employees grow.

When establishing a measurement system, managers should understand what their company's current state is and then set up rules and expectations. For example, if someone is spending five or six or seven or more hours on email and office applications, and one hour on personal sites per day,

he or she could be considered acceptably productive. Or not. It really depends on the management, which is why these guidelines need to be set within each department or the company as a whole.

Managers should have regular check-ins about goals and progress, just like any other critical KPI. For example, goals could include a 20 to 30 percent increase in sales, a least 20 percent satisfaction in support and 10 percent less time spent on entertainment websites. There should also be a plan in place for counseling employees who may be falling behind due to unproductivity. An employee's unproductive hours may result from spending too much time on non-work related sites or too many distractions in the workplace, whether in a traditional or home office. By identifying the areas where an employee is struggling, employers can work to help the individual reach heir full potential and grow as a professional rather than letting them go (and paying the cost of turnover).

Furthermore, with certain services, employees are able to keep track of their own individual performance and hold themselves accountable for fixing any problems. When they are able to visualize where wasted time comes from, it becomes much easier to focus on eliminating those distractions. It can also create a gamification effect of sorts – "how productive was I today, and did I beat yesterday's measurement?"

4. Calculating for brain break time.

Although understanding and monitoring employee productivity is critical to the overall health of a company,it

is important for managers to acknowledge that everyone is human, and we all need a break from time to
time. Short breaks (and vacations) have been proven to help the brain function better. As such, it is perfectly reasonable to allow employees some latitude in conducting personal business while on a work computer.

5. Give them a reason to believe your employees' any decisions.

Your employees are part of something bigger than themselves, but do they know it? From the first interview, potential candidates need to understand and share
in the vision of what you are doing as an organization. That vision alone will motivate and inspire your team, down to its junior members, which comes back full circle in effectively facilitating company growth.

For one company, as an example, the company's true purpose is "Improving Lives" as every team membe is aware. The team is directly improving the lives of the individuals they provide massage therapy
for, but is also improving the lives of HR teams by administrating the entire massage program fully, leaving them free to do their own jobs. Additionally, they improve the lives of CEOs and stockholders by improving employee retention and morale and decreasing worker's comp claims and health insurance cost.
And they improve the lives of people in local communities by helping businesses succeed, which improves the local economy .

6. Show you care.

Recognize every single employee's birthday. Send gifts for new babies and weddings.Be involved in employees' lives to let them feel loved and valued not only as employees, but also a family members and as human beings. "When people are loved, they will give more than you can imagine

they could for you and your cause," Wilcox says. In her company, she sends gifts to employees around every possible event in their lives. "Employees are the lifeblood of our operation. We want to make

taking care of them our highest priority and to make sure they are ridiculously happy at all times."

7. Recognize the good performance to some

performance excellent employee or appreciate their performance by benefit encouragement.

When someone is doing something awesome, tell them. Recognize the individuals on your team who receive good feedback from your clients. It's important for employees to feel their efforts are being recognized, and the recognition further perpetuates their desire to go above and beyond for your clients,

which of course, sets you apart as an organization as well.

Your company may not be at a point that allows you to offer a competitive full benefits package. But you'd be surprised how far a few small (and inexpensive) benefits will go with your staff. Any companies need to give each employee a massage every month (other regional companies such as Property Solutions and Usana Health Sciences have jumped on board in offering this benefit as well). "We also provide a monthly wellness allowance our employees can use on anything health and wellness related," she says. "And we feed our team (with healthy food options) at every meeting."

8. Promote from within when some employees

performance are excellent.

When your employees see that there is room to advance their career within your organization, it speaks volumes. Find out what skills and talents the different members of your crew possess and find ways

to develop those skills for future use in your business. When you have a stellar team member, help invest in the training they need to advance as your company grows.

Promotion from within can bring on the fun. An organization that plays together stays together.Even as a smaller organization,

(Single team members can bring friends and roommates instead.) A bounce house, live band, face painting, food and dancing prevail. For the holidays, the company hosts a fancy dinner and movie premier night

for each employee plus one. These celebrations acknowledge to employees that the organization can't succeed without them.

In conclusion, every organization leaders and school teachers also have responsibilities to raise their students or employees' mind management training skills, instead of students or working people learn mind management skills by themselves, if they hope that every student or working person can raise working efficiencies or learning performance more effectively.

THE RELATIONSHIP BEHAVIORAL MIND AND RAISING ANALYTICAL AND LEARNING ABILITY

What does behavioral mind mean?

Some behavioral psychologists explain behavioral mind means that in behavioral therapy, the goal is to reinforce desirable behaviors and eliminate unwanted or maladaptive ones. Behavioral therapy is rooted in the

principles of behaviorism, a school of thought focused on the idea that we
learn from our environment. The techniques used in this type of treatment are based on the theories of classical conditioning and operant conditioning.

One important thing to note about the various behavioral therapies is that unlike some other types of therapy that are rooted in insight (such as psychoanalytic and humanistic therapies), behavioral therapy is action-based. Behavioral therapists are focused on using the same learning strategies that led to the formation of unwanted behaviors. Because of this, behavioral therapy tends to be highly focused. The behavior itself is the problem and the goal 'is to teach clients new behaviors to minimize or eliminate the issue. Old learning led to the development of a problem and so
the idea is that new learning can fix it.

There are also three major areas that also draw on the strategies of behavioral therapy:
Cognitive-behavioral therapy relies on behavioral techniques but adds a cognitive element, focusing on the problematic thoughts
that lie behind behaviors. Applied behavior analysis utilizes operant conditioning to shape and modify problematic behaviors.
Social learning theory centers on how people learn through observation. Observing others being rewarded or punished for their
actions can lead to learning and behavior change.

Does good behavioral mind influence analytical ability ?

Analytical thinking skills are critical in the work place because they help you to gather information, articulate, visualize and solve complex problems. Even with comprehensive training, there will be many times where you will be put on the spot to think analytically and the right or wrong answer could make a difference with regard to your upward mobility within the company.

You want your employees and especially your boss to trust that you will make the most well-informed and correct decisions.

Some decisions can even make or break your career. Therefore, it is of utmost importance to have well-developed analytical thinking skills. However, where do you start? Sometimes, you need to use specific techniques to get information in and out of your brain, creating highly effective maps. This crucial online course will give you the tools you need for effective mind

mapping. Read on to learn more.

What is the different between Analytical Vs. Critical Thinking ?

Some people make the assumption that analytical thinking and critical thinking are one in the same. That is not actually true. You want to have the ability to differentiate the two so that you understand when you need to think critically and when you need to think analytically.When you think critically, you make the decision whether or not an event, an object or situation appears to be right or wrong. Once you are given information, you evaluate the data and determine how it should be best interpreted. You then make conclusions regarding your unique perception of the information. Moreover, you combine your new information with your current knowledge of the world in order to make the most accurate assessment you can make. You start to look into other pieces of data that could be relevant. In addition, critical thinking takes facts and uses them to form an opinion or a belief.

As for analytical thinking, you use it to break down a series of complex bits of information. You take thinks step-by-step to develop an overall conclusion, answer or solution. You look at something through different points of view with the objective to create a cause and an effect. To illustrate, you might try to determine why dogs wag their tails, and then come up with the scientific answer.Also, with analytical thinking, you use facts to support your conclusion and train of thought. On the other hand, critical thinking is more of an opinion-based style of thinking. Analytical skills lead you to have a more focus and stream-lined approach to solution finding where critical thinking skills can go around in circles infinitely. When you have a complex-problem or solution to find, you would use your analytical skills.

Can improve better behavioral mind to developing analytical Skills?

If you worry that your analytical skills are not up to par, never fear. They can be developed with time and consistent practice.

Like a muscle, the more you use it, the stronger it gets. One way to start is to read more books. This may sound a little too simple

of a solution but it really works. How does it work? Well, it helps when you read as actively as possible. Instead of passively skimming

over paragraphs and grazing the pages, try to look at both sides of the story. For example, if you are reading a novel, try to see

the plot from the perspective of the hero, the villain and other supporting characters. This causes your brain to think in new ways,

and increase your stimulation. Thinking differently helps to expand your mind, which is critical. To expand, this powerful online
course gives you recipes to help you with fresh forms of thinking.

Another excellent option is to build your mathematical skills. Calculus, algebra and statistics all make use of logic and analysis.
You need to go through each problem step-by-step in order to come up with the right answer. Sometimes, you have to work a problem
multiple times before you finally figure it out. This can be frustrating, but you get better with focused practice. You can also work
through different puzzles with the goal of solving them.

Analysis and the Workplace analytical thinking So, now that you understand the purpose and how to use analytical skills,
you might not yet know how it is used at your place of work. Well, there are several ways that may not have even crossed your mind.
For instance, say you have large amounts of numerical data that you need to summarize. In this example, you might need to use the Excel
program to plot the information, in addition to Pivot Tables.If you have a large, high-level project due in a few times, you are
going to have to break it down. First, you need to look at the big picture, and ask what purpose it serves and who it benefits. Second, you need to prioritize the steps you need to take and in what order. Third, you might have to delegate several parts of the project in order to get it done on time. Fourth, you will have to manage the progress and results of

the project.

Can mind influences human behavior and health?

People who have good emotional health are aware of their thoughts, feelings, and behaviors.

They have learned healthy ways to cope with the stress and problems that are a normal part of life. They feel good about themselves and have healthy relationships.

However, many things that happen in your life can disrupt your emotional health. These can lead to strong feelings of sadness,

stress, or anxiety. Even good or wanted changes can be as stressful as unwanted changes. These family or personal matters may raise your stressful feeling, they may include:

· Being laid off from your job.
· Having a child leave or return home.
· Dealing with the death of a loved one.
· Getting divorced or married.
· Suffering an illness or an injury.
· Getting a job promotion.
· Experiencing money problems.
· Moving to a new home.
· Having or adopting a baby.

Your body responds to the way you think, feel, and act. This is one type of "mind/body connection." When you are stressed,

anxious, or upset, your body reacts in a way that might tell you that something isn't right. For example, you might develop high

blood pressure or a stomach ulcer after a particularly stressful event, such as the death of a loved one.

Path to Improved Health

There are ways that you can improve your emotional health. First, try to recognize your emotions and

understand why you are
having them. Sorting out the causes of sadness, stress, and anxiety in your life can help you manage your emotional health.

If feelings of stress, sadness, or anxiety are causing physical problems, keeping these feelings inside can make you feel worse.
It's okay to let your loved ones know when something is bothering you. However, keep in mind that your family and friends may not always be able to help you deal with your feelings appropriately. At these times, ask someone outside the situation for help. Try asking your family doctor, a counselor, or a religious advisor for advice and support to help you improve your emotional health.

However, we need to live in a balanced life.
Focus on the things that you are grateful for in your life. Try not to obsess about the problems at work, school, or home that lead to negative feelings. This doesn't mean you have to pretend to be happy when you feel stressed, anxious, or upset. It's important to deal with these negative feelings, but try to focus on the positive things in your life, too. You may want to use a journal to keep track of things that make you feel happy or peaceful. Some research has shown that having a positive outlook can improve your quality of life and give your health a boost. You may also need to find ways to let go of some things in your life that make you feel stressed and overwhelmed. Make time for things you enjoy.People with resilience are able to cope with stress in a healthy way. Resilience can be learned and strengthened with different strategies. These include having social support, keeping a positive view of yourself, accepting change, and keeping things in perspective. A counselor or therapist can help you achieve this goal with cognitive

behavioral therapy (CBT).

You need often to calm your mind and body.
Relaxation methods, such as meditation, listening to music, listening to guided imagery tracks, yoga, and Tai Chi are useful
ways to bring your emotions into balance. Free guided imagery videos are also available on
Meditation is a form of guided thought. It can take many forms. For example, you may do it by exercising, stretching, or breathing deeply. Ask your family doctor for advice about relaxation methods.

To have good emotional health, it's important to take care of your body by having a regular routine for eating healthy meals,
getting enough sleep, and exercising to relieve pent-up tension. Avoid overeating and don't abuse drugs or alcohol. Using drugs or alcohol just causes other issues, such as family and health problems.

Does it have relationship between behavioral mind and analytical ability ?

Guilford's seminal studies (Guilford, 1967) propose that an average level of intelligence is required to demonstrate a creative skill. However, according to the threshold theory, in individuals with high levels of intelligence
(IQ ? 120) creativity is no longer related to intelligence. Studies that have explored this phenomenon have shown inconsistent
results. Most of the available literature has originated from Western countries find a between different measures of IQ and creativity. The goal of this study was to find a using tasks of analytical skills (verbal, scientific and mechanical reasoning) and creativity (fluency, flexibility, originality and elaboration) by conducting segmented regression

analysis in a representative sample of Saudi Arabian students.

The sample of 4368 3rd to 11th grade students (53.1% girls) was divided into three grade-groups (3rd–5th, 6th–8th, and 9th–11th).

A discover was found only for 6th–8th graders at a level of analytical skills of 108.8, and at 108.4 for 9th–11th graders. The analysis of gender differences showed that the threshold was significantly higher for boys than girls in the group of 9th–11th graders (105.6 for boys, 81.46 for girls). These discoveres were generally lower than those reported in other studies. Contrary to the relationship between creativity and analytical skills was positive and significant only above the thresholds. Potential factors accounting for these findings may be the type of analytical skills tasks, more related with crystallize intelligence and the culture-specific educational experiences of Saudi children.

IN conclusion, it seems that childrens' behavioral mind performance will implies that whether their analystical abilities are high or low. Also, it can conclude that childrens' high or low analytical abilities are influenced by their daily behavioral mind performance. It means that good or correct mind can cause correct behavioral performance to them. If one child can be taught to learn to observe any things or matters in the right mind by the teacher. Then, it will be influenced to them to raise high analytical skills or abilities in possible. It explains that if the person , e.g. student can have good psychological mind to attempt to judge to do any matters or anythings, then the student ought have high level of analytical ability or skill in possible. Then, when he has better analytical ability, he will feel easy to learn or it can encourage him to raise interest to learn.

Consequently, the student can raise learning ability in order to learn any new knowledge more easily. So, training high analytical ability , it needs to depend on how to train young people have good behavioral mind to judge anythings or matters daily. I believe that training better behavioral mind will be only the best method to raise student's analytical ability in order to let they feel easy to learn in education industry aspect.

Also, you might have to resolve a technical issue. Your first step would be to determine the cause of the problem. Then, you have to fix the error. After that, you want to take preventative measures to ensure it never happens again. All of these things require questioning, researching and analytical problem solving techniques. Without strong analytical thinking skills, you might come up with the wrong answers that could be detrimental to your workplace reputation. For more important steps, you should check out this article on analytical reasoning.

IV

Future social essential development industries

Future energy development prediction

Firstly, I shall discuss what is human future energy development prediction. In the future, we will face energy shortage challenge if we can not control our behaviors to waste any energy, e.g. driving vehicle gas, cooking oil, etc. natural resource energy will have shortage to be supplied one day.

Why will natural gas be one kind natural resource to be used by human? We need to know natural gas is as an energy source. On the one hand, natural gas can be extracted from coal, it can offer a number of benefits an energy source. Natural gas typically burns more efficiently than coal or oil and can emit less greenhouse gas at the points of extraction and combustion, natural gas has a role in supporting the journey towards lower or zero emission renewable energy sources. So, natural gas has these beneficial advantages to supply to us to use in the future.

On the other hand, it has direct use for a range of purposes, such as heating and for powering fast-response, electricity, generation turbines. For example, Australia has abundant resource of natural gas. Gas can be piped to a liquefies natural gas (LNG) plant, where it can be processes into LNG for export. So, it seems that human future natural energy development will be coal seam gas developments are associated with a range of social, environmental and economic positive impacts are bought from natural gas energy.

Hence, different countries have regulation of natural gas development. The regulation of natural gas operations in undertaken by relevant state and environmental authorities. These authorities establish regulatory frameworks based on the evaluation of potential environmental risks and hazards of proposed developments. These authorities are applying comprehensive science, it can give insights into the likely risks and impacts associated with individual natural gas operations.

Predicting future natural gas energy how to impact human's environmental, economic, social development as below:

In fact, predicting long-term impacts of natural gas production can be difficult, due to potential cumulative and region-specific impacts of multiple developments. However, I believe all these impacts will be positive and bring benefits to human development. Moreover, estimating social and economic and environmental impacts for a given time and place is challenging because of these variation such as below:

(1) How to allocate nature of land use in surrounding area? Due to natural (gas) energy exploration is needed to seek any lands which have possible to own any kinds of natural resource to manufacture natural gas. So, environment protection is needed when any lands are explored to manufacture natural gas to the amount, density and location of surface infrastructure are required to explore geology, hydrodynamics economics and logistics of producing and transportation that the natural gas products are required.

(2) It will create transportation, industry job chance. Also, the range of management and monitoring practice how to operate natural gas companies. Hence, on one hand, natural gas product will bring environment pollution or natural land shortage challenges, but on the other hand, it will create any jobs (occupations) which are related to natural gas industry development. In the future, long term our societies will accept to use natural gas to replace other energy, when it is invented to be popular energy to be future used successfully. So, human needs to concern how to explore natural gas to avoid environment pollution cause to influence our drinking water to be polluted or air pollution or farming lands are polluted to grow any bad vegetables or fruits.

(3) I shall indicate one kind of natural gas, e.g. ground water energy. Modelling of ground water systems can help to predict potential impacts of natural gas development. Modelling large ground water system, such as the great artesian basins is challenging, due to the size of the basins and scarcity of ground water date in sparsely populated regions. However, the principle of hydrology are needed

to understand. Insights into ground water behavior have been gained by analyzing the impact of historical water extraction.

1.1 How can future natural gas energy underground water energy exploration impact our natural environment?

The potential environmental impacts which will depend on the volume and quality of produced water energy. In the future, when we attempt to explore any natural water resources, we need to consider (water quantity and quality) both aspects as below:

Firstly, on water quantity aspect, large amounts of water are produced, it depends on the site, the removal of large quantities of water may affect the levels and flow of ground water in surrounding. Because when human explore any ground water natural resource to manufacture when natural gas power (energy), it will cause that we will reduce fresh water to be supplied to US to drink, due to these places of ground water is applied to manufacture natural water gas.

Secondly, on water quality aspect, other challenge human will face water quality is worse, due to ground water is explored to manufacture natural water power. Hence, natural water power exploration will cause underground water quality is worse to manufacture drink water. I shall recommend following treatment of extracted water to remove salts and balance acidity. The potential impacts of this water on agricultural production and ecosystem function are likely to be manageable, e.g. through appropriate mechanisms for its use or disposal. It treated and used appropriately the water can potentially be used as a resource for agriculture, instead of drinking water or natural water power functions.

1.2 What will be social impacts from natural ground water power exploration?

This development's impacts include the access and use of land and water resources, competing demands placed on human capital to explore underground water power. The rapid growth relatively high income residents can result in a sharp increase in competition among residents for social and natural resources. This can create tensions at local and regional schemes.

So, negative and positive impacts will occur during future human attempt to explore natural groundwater resource to manufacture power (electricity). It will also alter the distribution of health to different stakeholders and regions and influencing the local availability of natural and social resources, such as water or housing development.

Consequent, how to develop future natural resource in economic view point, due to natural resource is shortage, such as groundwater resource supply. Then, future human choose to explore groundwater to manufacture energy or power or electricity. We need to concern how to allocate groundwater resource is applied to either drinking water or agriculture or water power , electricity energy these there aspects of different functions to avoid any one of these three aspects will encounter natural resource supply shortage one day.

Future prediction for scientific computer industry development

Nowadays, it seems that computer technology development had changed fast from 1980 till to now. It had been invented to improve from traditional calculation technology to enter simple desktop computer stage, then it had been improved to enter laptop computer stage, even it had developed to enter (AI) artificial intelligent mobiles or robots stage.

So, electronic development will be developed to manufacture, such as robot machines to be applied to assist workers to raise productivities, efficiencies, improved service performance for future human's intention. Even, robots will be replaced to manual to drive non-manual vehicles or it could be replaced to manual to manufacture any products in future one day.

(AI) technology brings this question: If future human's life or jobs are controlled by computer, does it bring only positive impacts to influence our life, when we will become technological civilizations absolutely?

My idea is that (AI) does not only bring positive impacts to influence our life. My reasoning is technological development will also bring negative impacts, such as environmental pollution or exhaustion of resource or biological or nuclear bomb war occurrence will be possible caused , due to immoral human technological advanced development intention

The argument is more abstract, and it seems like this past, human had stable life when our life had changed to industrial society from farming society. So, in the past industrialization stage, it would only bring benefits to human. It brings these products to let us to use, e.g. radio, television, light bulb, telephone, phonograph, refrigerator, automobile, airplane, spacecraft, computer etc. These technological products are beneficial to impact our life. But, after industrialization stage, some technological products will bring negative beneficial disadvantages to impact our life if some countries leaders attempt to apply these products to control or dominate other weakness countries, e.g. nuclear power bomb weapon, genetic engineering (biological weapon, cell disease attack) invention. These weapons need have high technological invention to manufacture to compare past technological product inventions, such as the stages are from past traditional low technological bomb weapon invention till to nowadays high technological nuclear weapons ,biological cell disease attack war genetic engineering weapon invention.

Due to high technological invention, it bring these questions?

How can we guarantee that human won't apply new technological invention to bring weapons invention to attack other countries when human will become technological civilization from technological control or management or domination future one day?

Is technological development only bring beneficial development to us?

I shall explain why computers invention will be one main factor to bring new kind of weapon invention to threaten our future life. Although, we can not predict whether we won't have negative influences when our life are controlled or dominated by technology. If some countries applied technology to achieve to dominate other countries to achieve their aims. Such as numerical computer will be adaptive , iterative, exploratory , intelligent and the computational power will be beyond their wildest dreams. So their technological development behaviors bring negative impact to influence other countries' people life?

So, adapt is managed by the computer's intelligence issue will become more considerable matter. Computations intelligence ought only be applied to human cooperative aspect, it ought not be applied to human attack or domination or control between countries aspect. Such as nuclear invention ought be applied to manufacture new nuclear energy or nuclear gas to be used to push space boats or anyone of other nuclear energy pushed machines. It ought not to be used on bomb function.

Although, numerical computation technology will have possible to bring war weapons, it depends on how human choose to apply this new technology. We only need to change our mind not to dominate other countries. I believe technological weapons war would not be caused easily.

However, non- numerical computations should also bring positive impact influence human's future life. For example, we can image what is true of toilets will be type of numerical computations, e.g. artificial intelligence toilets invention. It can be applied to convenient to old elders or handicap people to use when they feel their activities are difficult, who need one artificial intelligent toilets to use at home or in public easily.

Even, artificial intelligent chair wheels invention which can let handicap people to sit to go to anywhere in long distance conveniently as well as this artificial intelligent chair wheel can save energy (power) to be used to go to anywhere for long time. They do not need to often charge energy and save money.

Moreover , artificial intelligent 3 D printer invention will help any products to copy different product's same images which are very similar. It can help manufacturers to reduce time and cost to manufacture any products in short time.

So, number computation technology will help human to solve problem at great cost and it is the range of future science and engineering important development to bring beneficial to impact human's life. I believe that the dream of parallel computing will be fulfilled. And it is hand to avoid the through that if parallel computing and the human brain are both on the revolution or development or innovation. Brain researchers make discoveries to transform our methods of parallel computing, or computer scientists will make discoveries that secrets of the brain.

Consequently, I believe that future one day, computer scientists can invent machine brains which are similar, even same to human brain's effort to learn how to do any human's behaviors easily. The most important concern is that whether future (AI) machine brains will be taught to learn how to do beneficial and safe behaviors from moral human's teaching or they will be taught to learn how to do damage or hurt and unsafe behaviors from immoral human's teaching. This issue is that future computer scientists need to concern. We need to wait when this numerical computerization first day is coming to develop or improve our standard of life from (AI) machine brain's beneficial assistance.

Future biotechnology (reproductive science development)

Technologies drive change to printing press, railroad, the automobile to develop to make modern life possible raising of our standard of life quality. So, technological development improve human's life style. For example, we can apply 3 D printer to copy any new products, we can catch prior high speed railway to go to anywhere in short time fast. We can apply artificial intelligent mobile to link internet or take photos, typing, instead of common telephone communication function, even, we can catch artificial intelligent vehicles which do not need manual driving to go to anywhere auto driving safely. All those technological development aims to raise our old outdated products' efficiencies and performance to satisfy human's needs.

I shall research what will be future genetic engineering (biotechnology) technology and cognitive development to be improved to satisfy future human needs and raise standard of life in this aspect as below:

Genetic engineering is one kind of reproductive technology, biotechnology and computer science, human cloning science subjects consist, which will become feasible and safe to be used in popular. Human hopes to apply this kind of reproductive technology to create new intelligent species. Human's reproductive technology research aims to reflect humanities and the social and natural sciences in these several aspects as below:

Firstly, the feasibility and safety of reproductive technologies related to directed evolution, including but not limited to germ-line gene engineering, human somatic cell cloning and computer interfaces with the central nervous system. Secondly, achieving the social factors that can likely affect the adoption of reproductive technology. Finally, achieving the consequences of adoption for the individual, the family, the nation and the world to accept reproductive technology.

In fact, reproductive technology can bring beneficial to humans, e.g. reproductive cow or sheep or pig animals, it can raise these animals meats to achieve the best taste and more health and more fresh and large meat size to provide to human to eat; reproductive fruits, e.g. reproductive orange, apply, banana, reproductive vegetable, tomato, potato etc. food which can raise the more fresh and health and large size to achieve the best taste food to provide human to eat. So, reproductive technology can be applied to reproductive food or fruit aspect. It aims to raise food or fruit taste to be the best, improves more health food and fruit eating quality and increases food and fruit size to be larger and increases food or fruit number to avoid food or fruit shortage crisis. Hence, we can ensure reproductive technology can be applied to food or fruit improvement aspect to bring human's health .

The challenge of reproductive technology development is only that whether human chooses how to apply reproductive technology. For example, if human applied DNA text of several human beings. We applied DNA to gain the ability to manipulate in organisms which only one reproductive human being aspect. It is wrong reproductive technology invention intention to be applied to reproductive human being. Because every human is individual being, every of us has different personal characteristics and interest and behavior. We do not ought attempt to apply reproductive technology to reproduce another one same human being.

However, reproductive animals, e.g. cow, pig, sheep etc. It is legal and moral because reproductive these animals can increase meats to supply to human to eat as well as reproductive fruit, e.g. vegetable, tomato, potato, banana, orange, apple which can be raised taste and increased size and health fruit or food quality to let human to eat. So, I agree reproductive biotechnology ought be applied to reproductive food or fruit aspect, which ought not be applied to reproductive human being aspect.

For example, on DNA research aspect, if human can apply DNA test to research how to kill disease, e.g. skin cancer, cardiovascular disease, breast cancer, HDL, lung cancer, osteoarthritis etc. diseases. I believe reproductive DNA technology can help human to invent new medicine to kill any diseases in future one day successfully if human can attempt to apply reproductive science technique to reproduce any dirty rats to do any new medicine experiments in order to supply enough dirty rats number to let disease or cancer cell to enter their bodies to cause illness and attempts to let any new kinds of new medicines to treat them to research which kind of new medicines can kill these dirty rat's cancers or diseases successfully . Thus, I agree that scientists ought reproduce many dirty rats to do new medicines invention experiments to help human to kill any cancers or diseases to prolong our lives.

A major implication of future DNA , biotechnology, reproductive science development is that medicine will have to change in dramatic and essential ways. New medicine invention will move from a reactive mode to a preventive one. The most important human expectation is that future new medicine invention can kill any cancer cells or diseases. Thus, genetically modified organisms of reproductive biotechnology is expected to invent any new kinds of medicine to help cancer patients to kill any kinds of cancer cells, instead of killing other kinds of diseases and increase reproductive good taste and health and large size of meats and vegetables and fruits number to satisfy human' s food demand to avoid food shortage crisis.

Also reproductive human genetic technology can be applied to raise born child IQ effort aspect, if reproductive human genetic enhancement technology can be applied to build children who can be born with genetic advantages, e.g. raising foolish children effort can be raised more clever. It is the most important in the history of building clever humankind because it could change the every nature of the clever human species to let many foolish children have chance to raise their knowledge level to be clever.

Although, there is much debate about both the science and the ethics of human germ-line genetic engineering. Some scientists claim will never be possible to develop the technology for use in a safe way if the foolish children are attempted to experiment whether they can raise IQ effort to be clever from DNA, reproductive human germ-line genetic engineering technology. Also, many bioethicists believe that even if safety concerns are overcome, it is still unacceptable with a child's genes, whose brain development will possible be damaged or hurt to combat disease if any DNA reproductive human IQ raising experiments are unsuccessfully.

I shall argue that recent scientific advances are no doubt about future child IQ raising effort technical feasibility. The objections are raised by bioethicists are logically inconsistent or based on narrow religious beliefs. Instead, I believe that fundamental ethical is rooted in the conflict between individual autonomy and social equality. The nature desire of parents will expect their children can be more clever, so DNA , biotechnology IQ raising effort technology will have possible to achieve their clever children raising IQ effort expectation. I suggest every parents ought attempt to let their foolish children to an any IQ raising effort biotechnology experiment for clever human development to let they can attribute themselves knowledge to serve our societies if they can be raised IQ effort from biotechnology technology successfully.

Future health strategy development and life science predictions

Nowadays, we will face new diseases and new cancer cells attack. Human needs to concern our health. So, global health organizations will concern to develop new ideas, medical strategies, innovation and insights that encourage cooperation with the health value chain, connecting the public and private sectors, health providers and purchasers and consumers and suppliers to learn how to develop future healthcare and life sciences industry to satisfy future human health life need.

Nowadays, health and life industry is changing quickly, medical organizations need to understand how to respond patients' needs effectively and build a sense of urgency to assist patients' needs in the short time. The predictions for health organization development has these insights: satisfying to raise informed and demanding patents; new digitized medicine business model ideas; health tools application measuring quality of life not just clinical indicators. I shall indicate how to apply (AI) technology to bring beneficial to health organizations as below:

Health big data artificial intelligent gathering tool is pervasive requiring new tools and provider models. Medical organizations have good planned regulations reflect the convergence of health and life science to guarantee patients' medical safety. The networked laboratory partnerships cooperation and enough distribution can apply (AI) health big data artificial intelligent gathering tool to gather all patients' medicine need data from different medical organizations, clinics , hospitals which central (AI) health big data patients medicine record system in short time fast. It is the efficient distribution of large volume to value pharmaceutical medicines supply to satisfy different local patients need from medicine shops in short time. Single and global pharmaceutical organization has responsibilities to cooperate different kinds of enough medicine for back office supply to hospitals or clinics to satisfy patients' needs.

A new impact of (AI) patient's past medicine and health

care record service providing and medicine supply both cooperative business behaviors which can build hospitals, clinics and medicine sale cooperate reputation to satisfy patients' medicine and updated medical needs, due to their illness situation will often change, e.g. either their illnesses will change from good to bad or their illnesses will change from bad to good . Due to prediction of patient individuals are better informed about the diseases who have and might have and the availability of healthcare. Expectations of healthcare and better influences for themselves.

4.1 What are future global healthcare organization technological development strategies?

So, health big data artificial intelligent gathering tool will bring these beneficial to patients such as below:
The quantified self has prevented and is devoting time, energy and money to staying healthy. When ill patients demand specific treatments, they are also willing in part to pay. Patients are true consumers, they understand they have options and use information and data about themselves and providers to get the best treatment at a time, place and cost convenient to themselves.
(2) Healthcare organizations will engage with patients through social media and driving them to appropriate health products and health services for their budget and healthcare requirements.
(3) Online patient communities will grow and rich sources of crowd-sourced data with rating system for drugs and healthcare.
(4) Advanced technological analytics on patient chatter in these communities gather health information, providing a better understanding of which treatments deliver the best medical service outcomes, allowing real time tailoring of pharmaceutical messages and services. They also provide

early alerts on diseases, such as influenza.

(5) Medical health service and medicine sale both kinds of businesses and governments work with communities of patients, hospitals and payers to identify best practice and cost-effective treatments.

(6) New medical service provider and health industry models, including mutual and other forms of collaboration and cooperation help decrease costs and improve care.

(7) Persuading or encouraging consumers accept that they are largely responsible for their health, e.g. smoking consumers' incentive for good behavior for reduction in co-payments to lower taxes.

(8) Privacy and security of data remain concerns , but there is an understanding of the benefits of sharing data.

(9) Medical payers and medical providers have complex patients, have invested in analytical and program that lead to new care pathways.

(10) Clinicians need to engage with electronic health information from wearables to achieve engagement in developing and improving the technology.

(11) Most patients in developed countries now have effort access to their own electronic health records and decide who to share.

In the future, the new social media departments will learn how to achieve in supporting key brand launches. The department was only responsible for helping with patients and payers understand that not only was the efficacy of the drug and medical health service package superior to the previous care packages. It also encouraged the right behavior charge in patients, creating long lasting health, and thus cost benefits. It was also responsible for building a new form of trust between patients, doctors and the pharmaceutical company.

Consequently, future medical service organizations, governments, pharmaceutical sale organizations which need to cooperate to achieve effective and efficient medicine service strategies to achieve raising medical service performance to patient consumers. It is one important medical health service influential method to provide excellent medical service to reduce patient individual life dangerous risks and to save every patient's life to shorten their health time. Hence, future medical health strategy is one important factor to prolong patient's life by efficient medical health service provision. Hence, (AI) big data gathering record system will help many health or medical clinics, hospitals, medicine sale shop organizations have enough medicine number to prepare to supply the most suitable medicines to every patient to eat to treat whose illness in the most short time.

V

What are the differences between developing and developed countries

I shall explain the difference between developed and developing countries characteristics as below:

Countries are divided into two major categories by the United Nations, which are developed countries and developing countries. The classification of countries is based on the economic status such as GDP, GNP, per capita income, industrialization, the standard of living, etc. Developed Countries refers to the soverign state, whose economy has highly progressed and possesses great technological infrastructure, as compared to other nations. The countries with low industrialization and low human development index are termed as developing countries. Developed Countries provides free, healthy and secured atmosphere to live whereas developing countries, lacks these things.

The characteristics between developing and developed countries may include as below:

Developed countries means that a country having an effective rate of industrialization and individual income is known as Developed Country. Otherwise, developing Country is a country which has a slow rate of industrialization and low per capita income. Developed countries have low unemployment and poverty, developing countries have usually high unemployment and poverty. developed countries have low infant mortality rate, death rate and birth rate is low while the life expectancy rate is high. Otherwise, developing countries have high infant mortality rate, death rate and birth rate, along with low life expectancy rate. Developed countries have better living conditions and high standard of living, but developing countries have bad living conditions and low standard of living. Developing countries have high GDP from industrial sector income source, otherwise, developed countries have high GDP income from service sector income source. Developing countries have high industrial growth. Otherwise, developed countries, they rely on the developed countries for their growth. Developed countries have high equal of distribution of income, otherwise, developing countries have high unequal of distribution of income. Finally, developed countries have effectively utilized to factors of production, otherwise, developing countries have ineffectively utilized to factors of production. Overall , any thing of developed countries are better than developing countries in nowadays societies.

Between developed and developing countries, one can identify a variety of differences. This differentiation of countries, as developed and developing, is used to classify countries according to their economic status based on per capita income, industrialization, literacy rate, living standards, etc.

What are Developed Countries?

They have usually these similar characteristics as below:

(1) Developed countries have industrial growth and enjoy flourishing economy. Developed countries experience marked development and growth in the areas such as transportation, business, and education. Developed countries are characterized by a low death rate and low birth rate as well. There is usually a very small gap between the two rates in developed countries.

(2) Developed countries are not characterized by shortcomings. They are well-developed in all fronts and are served well by water supplies, amenities, educational institutions, health care concerns. This is because of the fact that people are endowed with awareness about every possible aspect relating to human existence. The absence of shortcomings in the developed countries is possibly due to the fact there is a low birth rate in these countries. Nutrition is available in plenty to mothers and infants in developed countries.

What are Developing Countries?

They have usually these similar characteristics as below:

(1) Developing countries depend on the developed countries for help to establish their industries. They have only begun to taste the growth of the economy. Developing countries

are in the beginning stages of development in the areas of education, business, and transportation.

(2) Developing countries are characterized by many shortcomings. These shortcomings include less awareness regarding matters relating to health, poor amenities, shortage in water supply, shortcoming in the area of medical supply, a higher rate of birth rate. The most important and worrying factor in the developing countries is the factor of poor nutrition. Poor nutrition to both mothers and infants is the main concern in the developing countries. Due to high birth rates, the probability of natural diseases is more in developing countries. Hence, the death rates are also eventually high in developing countries. However, since natural diseases increase by high rates in the developing countries, they will have a short population doubling time. In the case of developing countries, there is usually a big gap between the birth rate and the death rate. Infant mortality factor is influenced by the development factor of countries. A developing country for that matter would have higher infant mortality than a developed country.

Overall, economists will differ their different characteristcs from these several aspects as below:

Developed countries display a high level of development. Developing countries: Developing countries display a lower development in different areas such as industrialization, human capital, etc. Developed countries have industrial growth. Developing countries depend on the developed countries for help to establish their industries. Developed countries enjoy flourishing economy. Developing countries begin to taste the growth of the economy. Developed countries experience marked development and growth in the areas such as transportation, business, and education.

Developing countries are in the beginning stages of development in the areas of education, business, and transportation. Developed countries are characterized by a low death rate and low birth rate as well. There is usually a very small gap between the two rates in developed countries. In developing countries there is usually a big gap between the birth rate and the death rate. Hence, in overall, any aspects are worse, slow growth to developing countries compare to developed countries.

What are general their GDP difference

Developed Countries:

A developed nation is one that has a very high rank in industrial advancement, constructs its economy in light of innovation and assembling rather than agribusiness. The variables of production, for example, human and regular assets are completely used bringing about an increment underway and utilization which prompts a very high rank in per capita salary. A nation with a more Human Development Index (HDI) is viewed as a developed nation. It not just measures the financial improvement and GDP of a nation additionally its instruction and future.

Developing Countries:

A developing nation is those having a way of life or level of modern advancements well beneath that conceivable with money related or specialized guide; a nation that is not yet exceptionally industrialized. A country having less utilization of resources and low income per capita which leads to low GDP of a country.

Developed VS Developing Countries will have different development or growth speed to compare as below:

?Industrial Economies:

In developed countries, economy depends on industrial sector instead of agriculture sector. There is more development in industrial sector. In developing countries, mostly economy depends on agriculture sector and they are moving toward industrialization.

?Citizens:

In developed countries, citizens and well off and rich. In developing countries, proportion of rich citizens is very low.

?Unemployment:

In developed countries, there is no such issue of unemployment. They provide many employment opportunities to the citizens. In developing countries, issue of unemployment is there and it affects the economy of country very badly.

?Education:

The growth rate in education sector is very high in developed countries and they have best education systems. Whereas the growth rate of developing countries in education sector is low as compare to developed countries. While developing countries are following the education system of developed countries to achieve the standard.

?Technological advantages:

In developed countries, every place is full with technological advancements and they always try to make it better. In developing countries, there are many undeveloped rural areas and even urban sector have less technological advancements.

?Roads:

Developed countries have a very sound infrastructure by having better roads, railway tracks, airports etc. Developing countries don't have a sound infrastructure as compare to developed countries.

?Government:

There exists stable government in developed countries so that they make effective and reliable policies for better economic development. Developing countries have unstable governments and mostly try to following the policies made by developed countries.

?Health care:

In developed countries, good and better facilities for health have been provided to citizens. In developing countries, health care facilities are not so good and acceptable.

?Resources:

In developed countries, the natural and human resources are fully and efficiently consumed. In developing countries, many of the natural resources are still untouched and others resources are also not fully utilized.

?Income:

There is a high level of income as per citizen living in developed country so that they have high GDP and GNP. Developing countries have low level of income as per citizen living in country with unequal distribution of income as that have low GDP and GNP.

?High Human Development Index (HDI):

In developed countries, there are best education systems and better health care and high income level so this leads to high value and ranking of HDI. In developing countries, there are low income level and fewer facilities for health care and low rates of education so this leads to low or middle ranking in HDI.

?Life expectancy:

In developed countries, due to better health care the life expectancy has been increased and they have low birth rates as well as low death rates. In developing countries, life expectancy is not so high but has high rates of birth and death due to less facilities and education.

?Water and food supply:

In developed countries, safe and clean water is supplied

with plentiful supply of food items and good housing condition. In developing countries, dirty and unsafe water is supplied with less reliable food items and poor condition of houses.

In conclusion, all our daily necessary need and social need to developing countries growth will be worse to compare developed countries in our nowadays societies.

How to measure the difference between developed and developing countries ?

The measurement factors between developed and developing countries may include as below:

(1) GDP factor

The classification of a country does not only depend on its income but also on other factors that affect how their citizens live, how their economies are integrated into the global system, and the expansion and diversification of their export industries. A developed country is one that has a high level of industrial development, bases its economy on technology and manufacturing instead of agriculture. The factors of production such as human and natural resources are fully utilized resulting in an increase in production and consumption which leads to a high level of per capita income. A country with a high Human Development Index (HDI) rating is considered a developed country. It not only measures the economic development and GDP of a country but also its education and life expectancy. A developed country's citizens enjoy a free and healthy existence.

(2) Industralization or Commercial aspect factor

The term "developed country" is synonymous to "industrialized country, post-industrial country, more developed country, advanced country, and first-world country." The United Kingdom, France, Germany, Canada, Japan, Switzerland, and the United States of America are only a few of those considered as developed countries. A developing country, on the other hand, is one that has a low level of industrialization.

It has a higher level of birth and death rates than developed countries. Its infant mortality rate is also high due to poor nutrition, shortage of medical services, and little knowledge on health. The citizens of developing countries have a low to medium standard of living because their per capita income is still developing, and their technological capacity is still being developed. There is also an unequal distribution of income in developing countries, and their factors of production are not fully utilized. Developing countries are also referred to as third-world countries or least-developed countries.

Countries are categorized according to their economic development. The United Nations classifies countries as developed, developing, newly industrialized or developed, and countries in transition such as Kazakhstan, Kyrgyztan, Turkmenistan, and the former USSR. The World Bank classifies countries according to their GNI per capita income: low income ($995 or less) and lower middle income ($996-$3,945); as developing countries with an upper middle income ($3,946-$12,195); and high income (above $11,906) as developed countries.

(3) The country citizen living of standard level

The classification of a country does not only depend on its income but also on other factors that affect how their citizens live, how their economies are integrated into the global system, and the expansion and diversification of their export industries. A developed country is one that has a high level of industrial development, bases its economy on technology and manufacturing instead of agriculture. The factors of production such as human and natural resources are fully utilized resulting in an increase in production and consumption which leads to a high level of per capita income. A country with a high Human Development Index (HDI) rating is considered a developed country. It not only measures the economic development and GDP of a country but also its education and life expectancy. A developed country's citizens enjoy a free and healthy existence.

The term "developed country" is synonymous to "industrialized country, post-industrial country, more developed country, advanced country, and first-world country." The United Kingdom, France, Germany, Canada, Japan, Switzerland, and the United States of America are only a few of those considered as developed countries.

A developing country, on the other hand, is one that has a low level of industrialization. It has a higher level of birth and death rates than developed countries. Its infant mortality rate is also high due to poor nutrition, shortage of medical services, and little knowledge on health. The citizens of developing countries have a low to medium standard of living because their per capita income is still developing, and their technological capacity is still being developed. There is also an unequal distribution of income in developing countries, and their factors of production are not fully utilized. Developing countries are also referred to as third-world countries or least-developed countries.

In conclusion, the measurement factors to decide whether the country is either developing or developed country. The factors depend on whether: whether the developed country is a country that has a high level of industrialization and per capita income while a developing country is a country that is still in the early stages of industrial development and has a low per capita income , whether the citizens of a developed country enjoy a free, healthy, and affluent existence while citizens of developing countries do not, whether the developed countries are also known as industrialized, advanced, and first-world countries while developing countries are also known as underdeveloped, least developed, and third-world countries. For example, The United States of America, Canada, Switzerland, Belgium, and France are examples of developed countries while India, Malawi, Honduras, the Philippines, and Rwanda are examples of developing countries as well as the infant mortality, birth, and death rates of developing countries are also higher compared to that of developed countries.

Why and how developed countries need
assist developing countries to develop

I think that we should help developing nations, But only to an extent. If we keep, And keep on giving them needs they will start to rely on foreign aid. I think charities are enough, But if the developing countries really need help then we give them help. But not too much, Basically they need to do something themselves and stop relying and take their own action. In exchange for our help maybe they could give us a bit of natural resources? Developing countries may need to be assisted, They may include these reasons:

Global resource is shortage to allocate unfair challenge
Nowadays, global resources are not equally distributed in different countries. Thus, there are those who belong to the developed nations while there are others that belong to developing countries. With these unequal distribution, it is significant that developed countries must do their part in helping those who belong to the underprivileged sector. It is true that rich countries have their own problems to worry with; Can we introduce aquaponics in developing countries when they don't have the resources that first world

countries have? In many areas, there is no electricity available that is needed for many aquaponics systems; developing countries require simplicity, reliability, and freedom from the need of grid powerhowever, it is still their responsibility to help the developing countries people need to solve resource can not be allocated fair problem, such as Afria is one developing country, many people are drinking drink water, due to drought , so they will not feel health and they will feel sick , even die. It is one example of natural resource of clean water shortage challenge to Afica. So, developed country, e.g. US , it has responsibilty to help African to drink clean water because clean water is allocated to supply to America people to drink in preference, due to global clean water supply is decreasing, but human number is increasing and clean water demand will also increase. If clean water is only supplied to US people to drink , even other developed countries people , they can drink the most clean water. The reason is because Africa people is poor or dirty or low education level or it is one developing country etc. factors to influence many African can not often drink any clean water. It is very unfair to this developing country.

In 2010, there were 925 million hungry people in the world; 19 million in developed countries, 37 million in Near East and North Africa, 53 million in Latin America and the Caribbean, 239 Million in Sub-Saharan Africa, and 578 million in Asia and the Pacific. This means that approximately 1 in 7 people are hungry. Protein- energy malnutrition is the most lethal form of malnutrition/ hunger. It is a lack of calories and protein; protein is necessary for key bodily functions including provision of essential amino acids and the development and maintenance of muscles. Bringing aquaponics into third world countries would help prevent this problem by providing fish as a main source of protein. Poor nutrition is the cause or partial cause for at least half of the 10.9 million child deaths each year.

The number of hungry people has increased since 1997 due to three main problems: 1) neglect of agriculture relevant to very poor people by governments and international agencies; 2) worldwide economic crisis and 3) increase in food prices. Children who are poorly nourished suffer up to 160 days of illness each year. Malnutrition affects about 32% of children in developing countries. More than 70% of malnourished children live in Asia. Undernourished pregnant women in developing countries leads to 1 out of 6 infants born with low birth weight; this means higher neonatal death rates, increased occurrences of learning disabilities, mental retardation, poor health, blindness, and premature death. There is enough food to provide everyone in the world with 2, 720 kilocalories per person per day, however many people don't have the land to grow or the money to buy the food they need for themselves and their children. 1 out of 3 people in developing countries are affected by vitamin and mineral deficiency.

So, I feel that aid has diverse results. It can both harm as well help development. Rich countries might be sidetracked in terms of focusing on programs that will spur development. Asian and African nations should create long-term plans that will reduce the dependency on aid, while rich countries should transition from traditional methods of giving support in new ways. Rich countries still argue on the premise that they cannot afford aid or that they are being over-generous. The main idea here is not that they are questioning the aid itself, but the development project. Rich countries must be on the poor countries aid as these people from poor nations face injustice and hardships that are often caused or increased by the programs and decision of rich nations themselves.

However, giving aid is not really an act of generosity. Aid purchases things that donors desire. These might include political support in exchange for the "goodies" that the donor has provided. Rich countries must show support to the poor by abiding on the social, environmental aspects. It can also include adapting to climate change by changing one's own consumption. Another is to accept fairer trade rules. Moreover, rich countries can show true generosity by undergoing changes in the manner of living for the past few decades. It would be fair that rich countries believe they are being generous when they give out dole outs or loose change when poor people around the globe are trying to live on a few basics while living under the system that rich countries have developed. It is a reality that there are also poor people in rich countries that are undergoing tough times. However, it is not ethical to withdraw support from people abroad who are more underprivileged just because there are poor people in rich countries that need help as well.

In fact, many argue that the poor countries that rich countries provide financial aid are doing better economically. It is possible that these countries are growing and catching up with the standard of living. Say for example, the annual income of India might have greatly improved. However, when one divides that with the whole population, each Indian just obtains $3 or less per day. This issue requires obtaining the correct facts not only on financial aid, but on the act of generosity in this world. Rich countries do have a responsibility of giving to those developing country people's living need because they can enjoy any benefits in preference when resource is shortage and global need is also increasing in nowadays societies.

Some developed countries have obligation to help developing countries

The rich have an obligation to help poor countries who were exploited by their colonial rulers. The United States had a head start with its vast natural resources. But many countries in Europe, such as Britain, became rich due to their colonial reign in Asia. They expanded their empire to include poor, resource-rich nations in Asia. They exploited the region's cheap labour, with workers getting little in return for their hard work. For Hong Kong , developing country and UK developed country. UK had obligation to help this developing country, HK before 1997.

Hong Kong was different though. Britain ruled Hong Kong for more than 150 years and I think both sides benefited. Today, the city is an international financial centre with a strong economy. But some countries did not benefit from colonial rule. For another example, IBM founder , Bill and Melinda Gates set up the Gates Foundation to help poor countries. We take a lot of things for granted. This cannot go on. A spirit of give-and-take is essential for world harmony. Developed countries may not be bound by law to help poor nations, but they have the responsibility - and the power - to do so.

However, developed countries should help less developed ones. But whether this is an obligation is a matter for debate. I believe the government of a country should be responsible for the well-being of its people. It is wrong to allow outsiders to influence the development of a country. This could lead to serious problems.

A developed country faces various difficulties when choosing who to help. First, its choice could leave a lot of people unhappy and damage its relationship with other countries. Second, allowing foreigners to have a significant influence on a nation could lead to negative consequences. Some donors do not have the best intentions. They could use their power for their own advantage. This could lead to corruption and financial loss in the less developed country. Third, a developing nation may become dependent on foreign aid. And some donors might charge a hefty interest for their financial assistance. This could pose a bigger headache than not receiving aid at all. Hence, rich countries have to be careful when helping poor nations. It involves a lot of politics so the rich have the right to choose the recipient and ensure the aid does not get into the wrong hands.

Rich countries have responsibilites to assist global economy development or balance economy development

When global economy is unbalance developing. It will bring the damage of kindly cooperation relationship , e.g. export and import business activities to develop our global economy in success. For example, China and America themselve trade war will cause these both countries' GDP export and import income loss, even global economy will be recession. So, rich country, such as US has responsibility to assist developing country, such as Afria, China, Korea, Taiwan to help them to raise business competive effort and bring long term export and import business cooperation and create many factory jobs to China, Korea, Africa, Taiwan factory workers. Then, they can build kindly business cooperative relationship to bring global economy benefit in long term. Then, our global economy development will succeed more easily.

The first rational basis behind donating to poor countries is the notion that all men are equal. Some may radically oppose this concept, noting that their countries should solely invest its own efforts to remedy impoverished sectors of the population. Given the spread of poverty and homelessness, some have arrived to the conclusion that aiding other countries is not in our best interest. However, this could not be further from the truth. As member of the human race, we all occupy an equitable status as global citizens, and nothing can detract from this truth. Centralise your focus on the relative needs of your nation disregards the ailing needs of the developing world.

The second consideration simply poses the question of why not? Although wealthier, developed countries are plagued by their own respective incidences of poverty and lack of resources, developing countries suffer greatly, in terms of their accessibility to medical aid, vaccines, clean water, and a number of other amenities that are gravely understated in importance. With this said, we must venture beyond the bounds of our own comfort zones, and aid other countries because we are lavished with such a bounty in resources ourselves. Another indispensable benefit of aiding impoverished countries. Foreign diplomacy can significantly aid the national security of any nation. And providing aid to a poor county can ultimately benefit us, improving our perception in their eyes, a cultivating a certain level of civility and coexistence that breeds peace, instead of war. The fewer enemies that a particular nation has, the better.

The final reason is simple. We should empathize with other human beings. Every day, countless children succumb to curable disease, malaria and a number of other pathogens that could easily be treated with outside aid. Both children and adults are sold into slavery and trafficked around the world. Of course, the lingering issue of starvation is a palpable one that still plagues the world today. With this said, we should uphold a noble standard that permits foreign aid for this very reason. One often hears the argument that it is all very well to preach equity but given the planetary emergency the world faces from the threat of climate change we must set aside the equity principle in the interests of humanity as a whole. This is a wholly specious and self serving argument. It reflects the sense of entitlement to an affluent lifestyle, based on energy intensive production and consumption, while denying the even modest aspirations of people in developing countries. For example, global climate changes to warmth challenge , it can cause developing countries people their health to be poor. In a densely interconnected and globalised world, it will be impossible to maintain islands of prosperity in an ocean of poverty and deprivation. It is not that developing countries are claiming the right to spew as much carbon as possible into the atmosphere without regard to the health of the planet. As the main victims of climate change– the impacts of which they are already suffering – they have a much bigger stake in dealing with this challenge. They are, in fact, doing much more than most developed countries, to adopt energy frugal methods of growth, conserving energy, promoting renewable power and limiting waste within the limits of their own resources.

Why and how developing countries people's poor health issue , it may influence developed countries businessmen income ? I shall indicate Africa , developing example , if African are health, then this country will have many workers to assist or help US businessmen to manufacture many products to sell to different countries in short time. If US businessmen hope to pay the low wage to reduce their long time expenditure, Afrian must need have health to do any hard jobs in factories. If US businessmen only feel Chinese workers can help them to do any low wage jobs in factories, when China have many new businesses develop to pay better wages to employ themselves Chinese workers. Then, many Chinese workers may choose to help themselves China employers to do the factory jobs to replace US employers. So, if US can help many African have health to work, it may bring uncounted long time benefits to US businesses. Hence, such as this case, it explains why rich people need to help developing countries to solve health challenge.

Methods developing countries can become developed countries

Main industries aspects need to develop

How can developing countries develop to be developed countries in success? What the difficulties to them , that they will need to solve in this development process ? In today's sophisticated society,people of the developing countries are still fighting for their basic righs such a better healthcare,proper education and a sound source of income.While the governments of the underdeveloped countries are struggling to improve the living standards of their people,I believe that contribution by richer nations should be more in this regard. To begin,all human beings should help each other.Govenments of richer nations can take many steps to improve the living standard of the poorer naions. I shall indicate these aspects that they need to concentrate on solving in order to achieve developed countries in success as below:

(1) Healthcare development

Firstly,in the field of healthcare,developed countries can support he underdeveloped in many ways.They can send their expert doctors to train the medical staff in the developing countries.Also,they can open free medical camps in the selected areas of poor countries.In this way free medical advice could be given.Such camps can also start health awarness compaigns to make people aware of unhealthy lifetyle. Moreover, experts from the developed countries can also help with the vaccination programmes in the developing countries.This will led to decrease in infant mortality rate.

(2) Educational development

Secondly,assistance in the field of education should be provide to the poorer nations.The developed countries can provide funds to open new schools and polytechnic institutions.These will not only increase the literacy rate,but will also provide vocational education.Furthermore,the rich governments should provide the students of poor countries an oportunity to study in the prestigious institutions by giving scholarships.This will promote poor people to gain higher education.

(3) Promoting free trade development

Finally,rich nations should help to improve the economy of poor countries.This can be done by promoting free trade.This wil reduce barriers to international trade such as tariff,import quotas and export fee and will help to lift the developing countries out of poverty. To conclude,if we want to live in a beter world with peace and harmony,we should always help each other.Therefore,I believe that richer nations should help the poor countries in all the fields.

The challenges are needed to solve in development process

During the development process, they developing countries will need to solve these challenges, the developing or underdeveloped countries (as they were earlier named) are poor due to them having the following common characteristics as below:

The developing countries may have these social challenges , they need to solve , such as :

(1) On social medical aspect

Closed economy/State Controlled economy or practice of socialism (which is in practice -one man/one party dictatorship). Low levels of literacy and esp. female literacy (less than 75% female literacy). Low health and HDI indicators (corresponding to the literacy levels). Low per capita income. High incidence of corruption, nepotism and kleptocracy.

The following is the path chosen by most of the former "low income/under developed/poor nations" to become developed (Germany & Japan post WW2, South Korea, Taiwan, Brazil, South Africa and China - some are still in process)- Economically liberal but politically/socially conservative regimes. Immense government spending (Keynesian economics) on - Infrastructure (Roads, Schools, Bridges, Ports, Airports, Power Plants, Hospitals and primary health centers etc).

(2) On international trade social aspect

Opening up the economy to international trade and foreign investments. Export oriented manufacturing practices, wherein the bulk of the population which was in the primary sector (agriculture, animal husbandry and mining etc) shifts to the secondary sector (manufacturing) and experiences corresponding increase in wages/income.

Application of procedures and rule of law on a gradual basis from the earlier arbitrariness which reigned supreme. The first step, in my view, is to make sure to have an honest and capable government that are committed to the development of the country and to the welfare of all people in the country. It is, in fact, the most difficult step to start with. Once we have a good and capable government, it is not so difficult to figure out or implement all steps necessary to make the country developed and prosper. On the other hand, having a corrupt, incapable, in other words, not only dishonest, but also stupid and foolish government means losing everything, no matter how abundance resource your country has, or how much foreign assistance and aids your country receives.

However, some economists believe that they are not "developing", but MAINTAINED IN PERMANENT UNDERDEVELOPMENT on purpose. Market, same as everything, functions in 3D, the 3rd is the income strata. The "progress" is not for all the strata. Every upper stratum solves its own problems at expenses of pushing the next inferior one downwards (vertically) or over the edge (horizontally). Spend a few minutes on a search engine and you realize that the term "first world" is meaningless when referring to economic development. For example, Ireland, Switzerland and Sweden are examples of third world countries. A first world nation is one that allied with NATO as opposed to the Soviet Union during the Cold War.

(3) On solving social poverty aspect

Poverty is the default state of man. Knowledge is what allows us to go beyond our physical and cognitive limitations. With knowledge you can create technology that makes our lives better. At a base level, developing nations need a smaller percentage of their populations working in sustenance farming. This could be achieved by increases in farming productivity which would allow other people to specialize in making other goods and providing other services. Essentially creating more wealth.

Uaually, developing countries lack enough farming technology, they can't specialize in something other than sustenance farming if 80% of your population farms with oxen instead of machines. This is where knowledge comes in play. Many developing nations have rich natural resources and commodities they just don't have the knowledge necessary to turn it into something useful.

To summarize in one word what is necessary for a developing nation to become a developed one it is knowledge. Any one developing countries need to answer these questions, before they decide how to solve these social challenges in their development process as below:

What developing country will become the next developed nation? Why do they are developing countries ? How can they develop to be developed countries ? How long will it take for every country in the world to become developed? What is the way to develop a country? Which countries are likely to be developed countries soon?

For example, Brazilians is one developing country, because this country has high crime rate and poor rate is high and inflation is high. These are its social problems. As soon as hyperinflation and out-of-control crime was solved, Brazilians brought their money back to Brazil. The starting point for Brazilians is patriotism and nostalgia. Even with all the problems of corruption, taxes, bureaucracy and poor infrastructure if given a chance to make real money within the country a Brazilian will leave better opportunities in the US. So, Brazilians need to solve these social problems if this country hope to become one developed country in success. The easiest way to develop is: when each and every person decides to learn as much as possible, and decides to behave like civilized persons, who have total respect for all other persons' physical and patrimonial integrity. It's that easy and simple. But, often, the easiest things in life are the most difficult to learn.

What a developing country should do to be a developed one?

The countries that developed the fastest often had the longest paths. If you compensate for that fact, then it becomes obvious that economic freedom is both necessary and sufficient. In particular, countries should avoid: socialism, i.e. collectivization of the means of production expropriation, i.e. robbing foreign investors of their properties autarchy, i.e. cutting all international trade. The less countries engage in these, the faster they develop.

How can a developing country become a developed country?

Well, you could study economic history and learn how the present developed countries attained their present positions. There are also several examples in real time: look at how China and India are moving their countries from third world countries to developed economies. Two other interesting examples: Several African countries are using primarily cell phone techologies for communication and bypassing the infrastructure requirements for hardline technology. Ireland is well know to have been deforested when it's forests were harvested for the coal and fuel requirements of industrializing.

Developed Countries need to help Developing Countries to increase their competitive effort in societies IMPROVEMENTS IN HEALTH, EDUCATION AND TRADE ARE ESSENTIAL FOR THE DEVELOPMENT OF POORER NATIONS. HOWEVER,THE GOVERNMENTS OF RICHER NATIONS SHOULD TAKE MORE RESPONSIBILITY FOR HELPING THE POORER NATIONS IN SUCH AREAS. Eliminate political tension by encouraging participation of all in the political, constitutional and economic processes. I recommend developed countries, such as US, UK can help developing countries to develop in sucess in these several aspects:

-Invest in infrastructure, education and health care.

-Encourage rural agriculture by providing agricultural inputs

and raising earned incomes.

-Raise levels of literacy

-Encourage the modern sectors of banking, manufacturing, retail,

and extractive industries,

-Provide adequate sanitation and clean water

-Open the countries to direct foreign investments

-Remove trade barriers to exports and imports.

-Reduce dependency on single sectors that is diversification .

Can bring global benefit when all countries are developed countries

1. How Globalization Affects Developed Countries
There are three perspective of globalization. Which are as : The Hyper globalist perspective: This says that economies are becoming Denationalized due to this government will lose it influence over the trade within its border. It will have both good and bad effects. The Skeptical perspective: it is kind based on myth that globalization will not help the under develop country as they do not perform a greater role in flow of trade and services in the global economy.

I assume that future one day, all countries can become developed countries. The globalization development effect will be caused by our global successful development. Does it means that globalization can only bring benefits ? I shall explain that when all countries can developed successfully.

Globalization ought not only bring benefits to our global societies as below:

Globalization brings people and businesses together through the international exchange of money, ideas, and culture. However, some critics say it adversely affects developed countries. Opinions exist on both sides of the globalization debate. Proponents claim lower opportunity costs, producing positive growth, and reduced market volatility. At the same time, opponents decry the reduction of domestic job growth, cost of mismanagement to countries and the world, and the stagnation of wages.

Conflicting Globalization Views

U.S. President Donald Trump, for example, has been very vocal on his views of globalization and has taken a protectionist stance when it comes to free trade under agreements like the North American Free Trade Agreement (NAFTA), calling for higher taxes on imports and fewer multinational trade agreements. He has also increased tariffs on foreign goods to discourage their importation and use. No matter how much economists are quick to extol the universal benefits of globalization, some politicians and other economist demonize globalization as a force that takes away domestic jobs. These conflicting viewpoints have created a maelstrom of opinions and policies across developed countries that range from extreme protectionism through trade barriers, like President Trump's example, to complete openness.

From an economic standpoint, globalization is typically defined as the increase in the global trade of goods, services, capital, and technology. This growth in trade has been especially acute between developed countries like the United States and emerging markets, such as China. There are many factors behind the increase in global trade.

European devastation after World War I and II helped to jumpstart America and an industrial superpower and exporter. Lower transportation costs have reduced the costs of trade, technologies have eliminated some barriers altogether, and liberal economic policies have helped lower political barriers to trade. While cost reductions have helped accelerate trade, the largest driver behind global trade is supply-demand economics and the desire to increase consumption on the part of both importers and exporters.

Benefits of globalization

The core benefit of globalization is the comparative advantage—that is, the ability of one country to produce goods or services at a lower opportunity cost than other countries. While the idea seems simple on the surface, it quickly becomes counterintuitive when examined more deeply. The theory suggests that two countries capable of producing two commodities at different costs can benefit the most by exporting the good where the comparative advantage exists. For example, a developing country may have a comparative advantage in producing cement, and the United States may have a comparative advantage in producing semiconductors. While the U.S. may be able to produce cement more efficiently than the developing country, the U.S. would still be better off focusing on semiconductors because of its comparative advantage. This is why globalization is powerful as a driver of global consumption between countries of all capabilities.

One of the major potential benefits of globalization is to provide opportunities for reducing macroeconomic volatility on output and consumption via diversification of risk. The overall evidence of the globalization effect on macroeconomic volatility of output indicates that although direct effects are ambiguous in theoretical models, financial integration helps in a nation's production base diversification, and leads to an increase in specialization of production. However, the specialization of production, based on the concept of comparative advantage, can also lead to higher volatility in specific industries within an economy and society of a nation. As time passes, successful companies, independent of size, will be the ones that are part of the global economy.

Empirical evidence suggests that a positive growth effect takes place in countries that are sufficiently rich when it comes to globalization. For investors and economies, globalization also provides the opportunity to reduce the volatility of output and consumption, since products and services can be imported or exported with greater ease. Fewer "bubbles" arise from a mismatch in supply and demand if the production of goods and services is more elastic. But, when all countries can develop to become developed countries, globalization developed countries which may also bring these disadvantages as below:

Drawbacks of globalization

Globalization is often criticized for taking away jobs from domestic companies and workers. After all, the U.S. cement industry will go out of business if imports from a developing country drive down prices, even if consumption increases. Small U.S. cement companies would find it difficult to compete and likely shut down, leaving workers unemployed, while the larger U.S. cement industry would likely experience a significant protracted decline.

A second criticism is the high cost of a comparative or absolute advantage to a country's own well-being if mismanaged. For example, China has become a leading worldwide emitter of carbon dioxide thanks to its comparative advantage in manufacturing a wide range of products. Other countries may have a comparative advantage in mining certain natural resources—such as crude oil—and mishandle the revenue generated from those activities.

A final disadvantage of globalization is the increase in wages for workers, which can hurt corporate profitability. For example, if a rich country has a high comparative advantage in developing software, they may drive up the price of software engineers around the world, which makes it difficult for foreign companies to compete in the market. The phenomenon of globalization began in a primitive form when humans first settled into different areas of the world; however, it has shown a rather steady and rapid progress in recent times and has become an international dynamic which, due to technological advancements, has increased in speed and scale, so that countries in all five continents have been affected and engaged.

What Is Globalization? Why and how globalization may achieve when global countries can develop to become developed countries ?

Globalization is defined as a process that, based on international strategies, aims to expand business operations on a worldwide level, and was precipitated by the facilitation of global communications due to technological advancements, and socioeconomic, political and environmental developments.

The goal of globalization is to provide organizations a superior competitive position with lower operating costs, to gain greater numbers of products, services, and consumers. This approach to competition is gained via diversification of resources, the creation and development of new investment opportunities by opening up additional markets and accessing new raw materials and resources. Diversification of resources is a business strategy that increases the variety of business products and services within various organizations. Diversification strengthens institutions by lowering organizational risk factors, spreading interests in different areas, taking advantage of market opportunities, and acquiring companies both horizontal and vertical in nature.

Industrialized or developed nations are specific countries with a high level of economic development and meet certain socioeconomic criteria based on economic theory, such as gross domestic product (GDP), industrialization and human development index (HDI) as defined by the International Monetary Fund (IMF), the United Nations (UN) and the World Trade Organization (WTO). Using these definitions, some industrialized countries are: United Kingdom, Belgium, Denmark, Finland, France, Germany, Japan, Luxembourg, Norway, Sweden, Switzerland, and the United States.

Components of Globalization

The components of globalization include GDP, industrialization and the Human Development Index (HDI). The GDP is the market value of all finished goods and services produced within a country's borders in a year and serves as a measure of a country's overall economic output. Industrialization is a process which, driven by technological innovation, effectuates social change and economic development by transforming a country into a modernized industrial, or developed nation. The Human Development Index comprises three components: a country's population's life expectancy, knowledge and education measured by the adult literacy, and income.

The degree to which an organization is globalized and diversified has bearing on the strategies that it uses to pursue greater development and investment opportunities. When all countries can become developed countries. They may bring the Economic Impact on Developed Nations as below: Globalization compels businesses to adapt to different strategies based on new ideological trends that try to balance the rights and interests of both the individual and the community as a whole. This change enables businesses to compete worldwide and also signifies a dramatic change for business leaders, labor and management by legitimately accepting the participation of workers and government in developing and implementing company policies and strategies. Risk reduction via diversification can be accomplished through company involvement with international financial institutions and partnering with both local and multinational businesses.

Globalization brings reorganization at the international, national and sub-national levels. Specifically, it brings the reorganization of production, international trade and the integration of financial markets. This affects capitalist economic and social relations, via multilateralism and microeconomic phenomena, such as business competitiveness, at the global level. The transformation of production systems affects the class structure, the labor process, the application of technology and the structure and organization of capital. Globalization is now seen as marginalizing the less educated and low-skilled workers. Business expansion will no longer automatically imply increased employment. Additionally, it can cause a high remuneration of capital, due to its higher mobility compared to labor.

The phenomenon seems to be driven by three major forces:

the globalization of all product and financial markets, technology, and deregulation. Globalization of product and financial markets refers to an increased economic integration in specialization and economies of scale, which will result in greater trade in financial services through both capital flows and cross-border entry activity. The technology factor, specifically telecommunication and information availability, has facilitated remote delivery and provided new access and distribution channels, while revamping industrial structures for financial services by allowing entry of non-bank entities, such as telecoms and utilities.

When all countries can become developed countries. In a global economic view, power is the ability of a company to command both tangible and intangible assets that create customer loyalty, regardless of location. Independent of size or geographic location, a company can meet global standards and tap into global networks, thrive and act as a world-class thinker, maker, and trader, by using its greatest assets: its concepts, competence, and connections. When all developing countries become developed countries, they may bring these beneficial effects as below:

Some economists have a positive outlook regarding the net effects of globalization on economic growth. These effects have been analyzed over the years by several studies attempting to measure the impact of globalization on various nations' economies using variables such as trade, capital flows, and their openness, GDP per capita, foreign direct investment (FDI) and more. These studies examined the effects of several components of globalization on growth using time-series cross-sectional data on trade, FDI and portfolio investment. Although they provide an analysis of individual components of globalization on economic growth, some of the results are inconclusive or even contradictory. However, overall, the findings of those studies seem to be supportive of the economists' positive position, instead of the one held by the public and non-economist view.

Trade among nations via the use of comparative advantage promotes growth, which is attributed to a strong correlation between the openness to trade flows and the effect on economic growth and economic performance. Additionally, there is a strong positive relation between capital flows and their impact on economic growth. Foreign Direct Investment's impact on economic growth has had a positive growth effect in wealthy countries and an increase in trade and FDI, resulting in higher growth rates.8 Empirical research examining the effects of several components of globalization on growth, using time series and cross-sectional data on trade, FDI and portfolio investment, found that a country tends to have a lower degree of globalization if it generates higher revenues from trade taxes. Further evidence indicates that there is a positive growth-effect in countries that are sufficiently rich, as are most of the developed nations.

The World Bank reports that integration with global capital markets can lead to disastrous effects, without sound domestic financial systems. One of the potential benefits of globalization is to provide opportunities for reducing macroeconomic volatility on output and consumption via diversification of risk.

However, when all countries can become developed countries, they may also bring these harmful effects as below:

Non-economists and the wide public expect the costs associated with globalization to outweigh the benefits, especially in the short-run. Less wealthy countries from those among the industrialized nations may not have the same highly-accentuated beneficial effect from globalization as more wealthy countries, measured by GDP per capita, etc. Although free trade increases opportunities for international trade, it also increases the risk of failure for smaller companies that cannot compete globally. Additionally, free trade may drive up production and labor costs, including higher wages for a more skilled workforce, which again can lead to outsourcing jobs from countries with higher wages. Moreover, domestic industries in some countries may be endangered due to comparative or absolute advantage of other countries in specific industries. Another possible danger and harmful effect is the overuse and abuse of natural resources to meet new higher demands in the production of goods.

In overall, when all countries can develop to become developed countries, they may bring these general benefits to influence our society to bring positive changes. They may include: Globalization activity doesn't only reduce trade boundary but it lot more effects like one country come closer to the economy of other country, it help in mixture of culture, it helps in transfer information and technology, increase group of buyer and seller of products and services etc. this are only few advantages of globalizations. Due to globalization trade is getting more interdependent and to protect interest of every nation W.T.O keep a close look over the trade of every nation. Due globalization many environmental threats are evolved every country is moving toward industrialization which increase global warming and it is needed to be checked. Social problem are also occurred like exploitation of labour, increase in child labour in developing nations, lack of powerful labour union etc this social problem are needed to taken care of and proper law should be made to avoid such kind of problems. As every things as has some advantages, it also has some disadvantages also.

Advantages:

New market for product.

Helps in growth of economy.

Increase in infrastructure.

Free flow of technology and information.

Reduction in poverty.

Increases in employments.

International body governs trade through its law, so interest of every country should be protected.

Disadvantages are as follows:

It brings competitions because of which small scale industries suffer in under develop countries.

Globalization lead to growth in infrastructure but on other hand it bring harm to environment due to industrialization, reduction in forest areas.

Due to globalization environment, labour, resource of under develop countries are exploited by develop countries. Poor trade union.

Lack of control over country economy by its governments.

Effect of globalization on developing countries or third world countries

The thinking of first world, second world and third world countries are given by U.S.A which place itself as the first world nation, European countries as second world nations and as far as third world country are concerned under develop and developing countries come under this categories. The third world countries are further classified as under developed countries and developing countries. In under developed, countries like Afghanistan, Nepal, Bangladesh, Nigeria, Bhutan, Pakistan etc comes this are the growing nations but as far as development of economy is concerned they are far behind. In developing countries, countries like China, India, South Africa, Brazil etc are included because this are among fastest growing nation after globalization has taken place. But under develop countries are not much benefited because of this globalization process. Rather than getting benefit they are exploited. In a sense, due to cheap labour these countries manpower is exploited and it natural resource is been taken away as we can take the example of china, china is investing a lot in African nation and on exchange of this it is utilizing its natural resources.

What influences to the countries like china and India has grown tremendously after globalization.

Before globalizations export of china was not very high but now it is one the global leader in exports and as far as India is concerned before India was accounted only for o.6 % of world export and now it is accounted for 1 % of world exports. Brazil has also show huge growth its per capita income has also increased. Countries like Bhutan, Malaysia, Indonesia etc has tremendous growth in GDP in past five years. Outsourcing has increased in these nations. Now India earns 51% of GDP from service sectors and its service sector is growing tremendously because of it excellence in IT sectors and this boosted up after globalizations. Now china earns major part of it GDP from export which increased after globalization. As far as Latin America is concerned Brazil has show tremendous growth in export, technology and manufacturing sectors. And now it is among top five of developing nations.

Effect of globalization on developed countries when all developing countries can become developed countries

Due to globalization the develop countries are moving towards underdeveloped countries like India, China, Indonesia etc for outsourcing their job to these countries because of cheap labour. Nowadays develop nation are coming to under develop nation for setting up manufacturing plants in these nation because of its availability of cheap and skilled labours. Due to globalization develop countries are facing intense competition from underdeveloped countries, competition in sense employment, exports, technology etc. Due to globalization developed countries are also exploit resources like natural resource, manpower, and environment etc. of underdeveloped nations. Also, due to globalization the dominance of developed nation is also reducing. The people of developed nation are facing intense competition for job from people growing nation like china, India, Thailand etc. now for FDI in developed nation are reducing due increase in the FDI in developing countries like china, Brazil, India etc. Thus, when all developing countries can develop to become developed countries in future one day. Globalization developed countries got new market for their products and services, and new place for their business expansions.

Development of "Regional economic" will truly help India to build viable economic future for its citizens.

Due to globalization various effect and development has take place which help india to build viable economic future for its citizens. Due Globalization to this the infrastructure of India has developed a lot because of which transportation, sanitary, hygiene, sports complex and stadium has developed a lot and still developing which will give better environment for future generation. Nowadays, foreign education institutes are coming to india which has increased the level of education. Export of india is increasing with each quarter which help to reduce the fiscal deficit and increase the GDP of the nation.

Nowadays more and more manufacturing industries are established because of which more employment is created and hence improving per capita income of the nation. Due globalization India is more concerned about the global warming and planning its growth in such a way that it could reduce it contribution in global. And it will be helpful for future citizens.

Regional economies help to reduce domination of developed economies on the developing economies.

Developments in regional economy will strength the self reliability of the nation which will help to reduction in the dependence on other nation. Development of regional economy will lead to increase in GDP, Standard of living, Per capita income of the nation. If India wants to emerge as supper power it has to develop it regional because it is the stepping stone toward it.

In conclusion, when all countries can develop to achieve developed countries. They will create development of regional economy to our global societies. Then, they may bring these benefits in possible. They may include: Development of regional economy will lead to reduce in inequalities of distribution of wealth, development of regional economy will lead to increase in metropolitan culture, development of regional economy will lead increase the contributions of every state in Indian GDP, development of regional economy will lead to reduction of poverty, unemployment and illiteracy.

2. Economic growth advantages and disadvantages

When all developing countries can develop to be developed countries, then it may also bring global economic growth. However, I believe that when global societies can have sudden economic growth in short time, due to all or many developing countries can develop to be developed countries in success. They may bring advantages and disadvantages both aspects as below:

Economic development can be describe as the development of economic wealth of countries or regions for the well-being of their inhabitants such as the improvement and innovation on the political, economic, and social of its people. Economic development and growth are totally different in terms which are used in economics. Economic development refers to economic growth which accompanied by changes in economic structure and output distribution. So, economic growth may be necessary but not sufficient to attain economic development. Thus, peoples always said that economic development is the problems of underdeveloped countries and economic growth to those of developed countries. Underdeveloped countries always face some problems such as low income, weakness of human resource and also the economic vulnerability. These problems also made the countries hard to attain the development of economic. However, for those developed countries, they do not face the same problems as what underdeveloped countries do, therefore, they are more easily to attain the economic development and treat it as an economic growth.

In addition, in the term of economic development is much more comprehensive because it implies progressive changes in the socio-economic structure of a country. Nowadays, the evolution of new technology is directly related to economic development. Without high technology in a country, it is hard to bring an economic development toward its people. Viewed in this way economic development involves a steady decline in agricultural shares in GNP and continuous increase in shares of industries, trade banking construction and services. However, economic growth just only refers to the rise in total output in a country; development implies change in technological and institutional organization of production as well as in distributive pattern of income. Hence, if compared to the goal of development, economic growth is much easy to realize. Between, we just need a larger mobilization of resources and raising their productivity by enhance it to be more efficiency and effective, then the output level can be raised and economic growth will occur. However, the development process is far more extensive than the economic growth. Not only a rise in output, it also involved changes in composition of output, and shift in the allocation of productive resources, and reduction or elimination of poverty, inequalities and unemployment. However, economic development is impossible without having an economic growth but economic growth is possible without an economic development. Growth is just increase in GNP but it does not have any other parameters to it; unlike development which can be conceived as Multi-Dimensional process.

Are economic growth and development worthwhile? Economic growth and development have their advantages and also disadvantages. Although economic growth widens the range of human choices, but this may not necessarily bring happiness toward people. Happiness is dependent on the relationship between wants and resources. People may become more satisfied, not only by having more wants met, but perhaps also by renouncing certain material goods.

Wealth may make people less happy if it increases wants more than resources. Furthermore, acquisitive and achievement-oriented societies may be more likely to give rise to individual frustration.

Advantages

Economic growth will decreases famine, starvation, infant mortality, and death; gives us greater leisure; can enhance art, music, and philosophy; and gives us the resources to be humanitarian. Economic growth will especially benefit to societies in which political desire exceed the resources, because it may prevent what might otherwise prove to be social tension that people can't take it. However, without economic growth, the desires of one group can be met when others expense on it. Lastly, economic growth can help newly independent countries in mobilizing resources to increase the power of a nation.

Disadvantages

Growth has its value. First, the disadvantage might be the acquisitiveness, materialism, and dissatisfaction with one's present state associated with a society's economic struggles. Second, liquidity, objective, and self-associated with economic growth may undermine the reliance on extended family system, in fact, the focus of the prevailing social structure. Third, economic growth, which depends on the rational and technological innovation and changes in scientific methods, often is the threat in religious and social authority. Fourth, economic growth often require more specialized work, which may be caused by more objective, accompanied more drab and monotonous tasks, more discipline, and a pair of process loss.

In addition, economic growth which follow by large organizational units are more likely to lead to bureaucratization, objective, communication problems, and the use of force were consistent. Economic growth and development of large enterprises with a manufacturer's products and services while demand increased, and urban growth, this may be is accompanied byrootlessness, environmental blight disease, and unhealthy living conditions, even in the narrow social values change and may ultimately lead to a new dynamic equilibrium that is better than the old static equilibrium, the transition could have some very painful issues. In addition, the political transformation, as rapid economic growth, may lead to greater concentration, stress, social disruption, even authoritarian. Therefore, even if the population seriously committed to economic growth, its implementation is not likely at all costs pursued. All societies must take into account that the conflicts with the maximization of economic growth and other objectives. Because it was want sits in high level positions, a developing country own citizens can promote the local production control to reduce the growth in the short term.

The question now is what will be weighed to achieve an orderly, stable society, and maintain traditional values and culture, and promoting political autonomy? Economic growth is the increase a country's per capita output. Economic development, economic growth has resulted in the poorest strata of the population or level of education, changes to improve the output distribution of economic welfare and economic changes in different structures.

Economic growth and development of Asia when all or many developing countries can develop to be developed countries

Nowadays, economic development in Asia shows high impact of economic development of this respective continent. Economy of Asia has taken an important part in the view of the world's economy. These continents have adopted one of the following economic systems such as capitalism, socialism, communism, and fascism. As we know, Asia is the largest continent in terms of area surface and also the population. Beside it, it is also the region with the highest growth rate. Below are Asian countries that contribute their economic development to our society.

Of all the Asian Countries, the only Asian country included among the industrialized countries is Japan. According to the International Monetary Fund, the country per capita was GDP 32,608 U.S. dollars or in 2009, the 23rd highest on record. Moreover, according to certain criteria, the term means that developed countries is the countries that having a high level of development. What standards and which countries are classified as being developed, is a controversial issue which surrounded by a fierce debate. Thus, economic criteria tend to dominate discussions. Countries which having per capita income and high per capita gross domestic product (GDP) will be described as developed countries. Another criterion is the industrialization; countries in the tertiary and quaternary sector-of industry leading will be described as development. Another recent measure, the human development index, which combines economic measures, and other measures of national income, life expectancy and education indicators, have become prominent. This criterion will define the development country as those very high (HDI) rating. However, many exceptions exist when the decision to "developed country" status is used to measure the subject. Countries do not fit this definition are classified as developing countries.

However, Taiwan, Hong Kong and Singapore are regarded

as newly industrialized countries. The category of newly industrialized country (NIC) is a socioeconomic classification which applied to various countries in the world by political scientists and economists. NIC is the nation's economy has not yet reached first world status, but in the macro sense, the development of the countries is normally faster than counterpart. Another feature of newly industrialized countries is that undergoing in rapid economic growth (usually export-oriented). However, the starting or ongoing industrialization is an important indicator of NIC. In many newly industrialized countries, may also be experiencing social unrest by major primary rural, or agricultural, populations migrate to the cities, where the thousand of laborers can be draw by growth of manufacturing concerns and factories. In the social development process, it usually shares some characteristic such as increased social freedoms and civil rights, strong political leadership, which switch from an agricultural to an industrial economy, the other common features, especially in the manufacturing sector, an increasingly open market economy with free trade and other heavy capital investment from countries around the world. In addition, the political leadership in their area of influence and lastly is they have lowered poverty rates.

I shall indicate China, Philippines, India, North Korea these developing country when they can become developed country , what it can bring global social change influence example. Moreover, as we know, the history and culture of China is their secret to improve their economy, even if it ruled and control by their state. Prior to 1979, China maintained a centrally planned or command economy. The economy of China with the large proportion is directed by the state which established production goals, controlled prices, distribution, and most of the economic control of resources. During the 1950s, all of China's individual household farms were collectivized into large communes. To support rapid industrialization, the central government starts to take large-scale physical and human capital investment during 1960-1970s. As a result, by 1978, nearly three quarters of industrial production generated by the central control of state-owned enterprises according to centrally planned output targets. Private enterprises and foreign invested enterprises are almost non-existent.

A central objective of Chinese government was to make China's economy relatively self-sufficient. Foreign trade was generally limited to those commodity which unable to obtain or receive the goods in China. The Government's policy to keep the Chinese economy relatively stagnant and inefficient, mainly because of where the profits of some enterprises and farmers to stimulate competition, in fact, does not exist, price and production controls caused widespread economic distortions. China's standard of living is much lower than those of many other.

In addition, India is contributing in business process outsourcing improvement for the information technology which has a significant impact for the economic development in South Asia. The Philippines is improving, because they help to remittances from abroad, they send money to their loved ones from overseas Filipino workers to improve their country. North Korea shows hammer and sling as a symbol for their communistic views of their economic system in Far East Asia. While South Korea shows modern technology that is influence from Western countries which results an improvement of technology in their designated countries. Indonesia is a Muslim country, the whole of Asia's largest population by the Dutch colony.

It is based on their banking and finance in the Islamic way of life. This is also the case in Malaysia was a British colony. After analyze the information of some Asian Countries, I discovered that they are facing several problems in economic development. First, they have low standard of living, low level of production, there is a rapid population growth, they having a high rate of unemployment, lastly, there are over dependence on agricultural production and exportation of raw materials and also the international trade.

Economic growth and development of Malaysia
According to the recent The Star's newspaper, Malaysia economic development is one of fastest and steady in global economic scenario. Malaysia GDP per capita has been estimated to be $15,700 in fiscal year 2008. This is a clear indication of tremendous economic development in Malaysia. Malaysia economy is a middle income country that has developed since 1970's. It was previously a mere raw materials producing economy, which has evolved now as a developing multi-sector economy. This growth bears testimony to impressive economic development at Malaysia. Prime Minister Abdullah, after coming to power in 2003, has tried to develop economy of this south Asian country by introducing value added production. He took a number of measures to introduce hi-tech technologies and encouraged investments in high technology industries, medical technology and pharmaceuticals. Efforts have been made by government of Malaysia to stop its dependence on export products. However, exports of electronics goods have always been a major factor in Malaysia economy. There has been huge profit accrued from export of oil and gas and it has been a major factor for Malaysia economic development. There have been huge profits from high

energy prices, although there was high cost of gasoline and diesel fuel. This, however, made Kuala Lumpur minimize financial assistance of government. It has been found that currency value of Malaysia has hiked 6 percent per year when pitted against dollar in fiscal years 2006 to 2008.

Model of economy development: The production function how can be influenced to change when many or all developing countries can become developed countries

In macroeconomics, the production function is a function which specifies combination of all input from the output. In the macro-economy, production functions are functions that determine the output of a company which entered all combinations of input. A meta-production function comparing the practices of companies that has to change input to output to determine the function of the most efficient production practices of the entity that is, whether the most efficient production practices that qualify or production practices that are actually the most efficient. In these cases, the maximum output production process technology is defined as mathematical function of one or more entered. In other words, given a collection of all technical combination allows the output and input, just include a combination of maximum output for a given set of inputs to the production or function. Production function can be defined as specification of minimum input requirements needed to produce a total output that was, by given current technology. It is usually assumed that the production of unique functions can be built for every production technology.

Assuming when many or all developing countries can develop to become developed countries in future one day, they may bring these influences to our social technologic production function changes as below:

The maximum output possible from the set of technology inputs of all, the economic use in the production function analysis is the abstract essence of the technical and managerial problems associated with a specific production process. Engineering and managerial problems of technical competence is assumed to be broken, so the analysis can focus on the problem of efficiency allocate. States are assumed to make choices about how much each input of allocate factors put to use and how much output to produce, remember the cost (purchase price) of each factor, the sale price of output, and the factors represent technology to determine its production function. Frame results in one or more constant input can be used, for example, capital can be assumed to be fixed (constant) in the short term, and labor and possibly other variables such as input raw material, while in the long run, the quantity of capital and the factors that can be made by the company are variable. In the long term, companies may even have the choice of technology, represented by the various functions of production as possible.

Input to output relationship is non-financial, that the production function relating physical inputs to physical outputs, and prices and the cost is reflected in the function. But the production function is not a complete model of the production process: intentionally abstract from the inherent aspects of physical production process that some would consider extremely important, including error, entropy or waste. In addition, the production functions do not typically model business processes, well, ignoring the role of management. (For primer on the basic elements of the production of Microeconomics theory, see production theory policies).

The main purpose of the production function is to address allocate efficiency in the use of input factors in production and distribution of factory income such factors. Based on certain assumptions, the production function can be used to reduce a marginalized product for each factor, which implies an ideal division of the revenue generated from the output to the income from their every input factor of production.

How global developed economy influences household expenditure decision?

In the saving function, there is a mathematical relation between saving and income by the household sector. Thus, the saving function can be stated as an equation such as a simple linear equation or a diagram indicated as the saving line. This function captures the relationship between savings and income, one of the other sides the relationship between consumer incomes, constitutes a cornerstone of Keynesian economics. The two key function to save the parameters are intercept, which indicates that self-saving, side slope, which is the marginal propensity to save, show that the induced savings. The injection- leakage model used in Keynesian economics is based on the saving function.

Saving function on Keynesian economics is the starting point for determination of equilibrium output injection, leakage model. It captures the household sector in which the relationship between savings and income. As the income for either consumption or savings to use, saving feature is the complementary consumption function. Reflects the fundamental psychological law put forward by John Maynard Keynes, consumer spending (and saving by the household sector) depends on the income and just some of the revenue is used for consumption and saving the rest. This function is presented either as a mathematical formula, usually as a simple linear equation, graph or savings line. In either form, income is a measure of disposable income, national income and GDP. However, the saving function makes it easy to divide saving into two basic types such as the autonomous saving and Induced saving. Autonomous saving is the intercept term. Induced saving is the slope. Lastly, the slope of marginal propensity to save (MPS) also considered as saving function

How global developed economy influences the labor supply function changes ?

In mainstream economic theory, labor supply is the total number of hours number of a workers want to work in a given real wage rate. From the diagram above, we can see the positive relationship between the wages rate and also the quantity of labor. When the wage rate is low, the quantity of the labor also is low. However, when there is a rose in wage rate will also increase the quantity of labor. Realistically, the labor supply is the role of various factors within an economy. For example, as a heavy increased of population will make downward pressure on wages which may lead to high unemployment.

How global developed economy influences wage rate versus labor leisure changes?

Labor supply curves are derived from the 'labor-leisure' trade-off. More hours worked earn higher incomes but necessitate a cut in the amount of leisure that workers enjoy. Therefore, there are two aspects, to provide the necessary amount of labor is due to changes in real wage rates. For example, the real wage rate raises the opportunity cost of leisure increases as the diagram shows above. This tends to cause workers to supply more labor (the "substitution effect"). However, as the real wage rate rises, workers earn a higher income for a given number of hours.

If leisure is a normal good – the demand for it increases as income increases – this increase in income will tend to cause workers to supply less labor (the "income effect"). If the "substitution effect" is stronger than the "income effect" then the labor supply curve will be upward sloping and vice versa.

However, from the view of Marxist, a labor supply is a core requirement in a capitalist society. In order to avoid Labor shortage and ensure a labor supply, a large portion of the population must not possess sources of self-provisioning, which would allow them to be independent, and they must instead be compelled, in order to survive, to sell their labor for a subsistence wage.

Economic development theories: Harrod-Domar theory When all or many countries can develop to be developed countries, how they can influence global technological growth rate changes. The Harrod-Domar theory delineates a functional economic relationship in which the growth rate of gross domestic product (g) depends directly on the national saving ratio (s) and inversely on the national capital/output ratio (k) so that it is written a $g = s / k$. The equation takes its name from a synthesis of analyses of growth process by two economists (Sir Roy Harrod of Britain and E.V. Domar of the USA). The Harrod-Domar model in the early postwar times was commonly used by developing countries in economic planning. With a target growth rate, the required saving rate is known. If the country is not capable of generating that level of saving, a justification or an excuse for borrowing from international agencies can be established. An example in the Asian context is to ascertain the relationship between high growth rates and high saving rates in the cases of Japan and China. It is more difficult to introduce the third building block of a growth model, the labor and population element. In the long run, growth rate is constrained by population growth and also by the rate of technological change.

Climate change will impact developed countries to continue develop

Will developed countries become
developing countries

Why does illness can cause global economic recession to developed countries

Firstly, I shall explain why unpredicted illness factor can cause developed countries' economic recession. Although developed countries have advantages and let people to believe that their any medical, economic, education, business etc. different industries aspects are developed in mature. Their these any industries aspects are better or are improved better to compare the developing countries. But, in fact, whether it is possible that their any industries aspects will become worse to compare developing countries when they do not continue to improve any one of their industries aspects. I shall indiate whether what factors my cause developed countries to become developing countries in possible.

Many developing countries are facing problem very different from that of the developed countries. Countries such as Japan, Germany are facing depleting population whether on the other side countries like India, Indonesia are facing severe resource crunch due to population explosion. In such situation measuring the progress of the countries on the same scales decided by developed industrialized world is injustice to these countries. Developed world have achieved there parameters after journey of around 200-250 years post industrialization while many developing countries are in their 60s-70s after getting freedom from crutches of colonialism. In such cases developing countries should formulate their own parameters for growth and development and continue their progress. So, it seems that any developing countries will have possible to develop to be better any developed countries. Otherwise, any developed countries will have possible to bring worse development when they have many people loss jobs. For example, US economy will go down nowadays, due to the Chinese serious illness influences many US people die. Many US businessmen can not continue to manufacture or sell their products because many people can not go to offices or factories to work. They need to stay at homes to avoid the illness attacks when they need to contact the illness people in workplace, or they are walking on streets, or they are catching any public transport. So,although US is one developed country, but it can not still to avoid this China illness attack. It is possible due to US government neglects to consider this China illness is one kind of death sick to cause US has many people to die easily in this year 2020. If US government can prohibit to let Chinese travellers to enter its country when China has occurred this serious illness caused in 2019 last year. These Chiness illness people can not enter US to cause this kind of illness to attack any US people lung to cause they die. After it is possible that US can avoid to cause many US people to die. So, it does not consider whether the country is developed or not to avoid global economic recession, because it is illness factor to cause developed countries' economic recession, such as US, UK nowadays economic recession.

Increasing social crime rate and government assistance may cause developed countries to become developing coutries

Secondly, I shall explain why increasing social crime rate or many young people do criminal behaviors in society, it can influence developed countries to develop worse or can not develop better in its society. Otherwise, when on developing countries have less crime rate or decreases its crime rate, it can develop better or improve its society to be better. For a developing country to catch up to a developed country, it must not only grow, but grow faster than the developed country. While It is possible for such accelerated growth to occur through rapid industrialization, but there are many country-specific factors that directly affect a developing country's ability to catch up to developed countries. They range from growth of productivity, labour force participation rate, standard of living, infrastructure, political environment etc.

For example, when the developing country can improve its education quality to let many young people learn any kinds of new knowledge to like do any kinds of jobs, even, driving , factory labor, waitors, etc. low educational level jobs in society. Then, it will reduce its crime rate when many young people feel need to work. They won't need government to assist their life. Consequently, it will have possible to develop its economy or improve its economy to be better. In education primarily is the most essential quality that helps to empower the people of the country to communicate and achieve a common objective and is thus an extremely important driver for the developing to developed country journey. This is a common observation in all the developing countries. The one area that is still a struggle is education.

Also, lack of education leads to increased poverty and disparity of income which leads to the 2nd most hindrance in a countries journey to achieve a developed nation status. Maybe if the path chosen is that of streamlining lack of education, poverty, a more driven and focused effort with individuals who know and can fathom the importance of this change working towards achieving a developed nation status can be undertaken. A semi-industrial, pro-human development approach should be a path adopted to see a qualitative shift in reducing this gap.

All through our education we have learnt 'India is a developing country' which brings to thought, will it ever be recognized as a 'developed country'? And what is the criteria to qualify as a developed nation? Are these criteria set by the developed nations to meet their convenience? If this is the case it would be more logical for developing nations to set their own criteria. It gets very difficult for developing nations to meet the criteria set by the giant economies, as even a single step gone wrong could ruin the effort of years. India can be seen as an example, where the step of demonetization and GST together led to a growth rate of 5.7%, weakest growth rate since the first quarter of 2014. These steps would probably have a positive effect in the long run and it is worth the wait. Another question to bring our attention to is, are the developed countries developed in the true sense? Considering the parameter of crime rate, USA has a very high crime rate. Another aspect could be unemployment, again US has a good percent of unemployed individuals every year. So, aren't the developed nations also falling short? It may be a good strategy for developing nations could be establishing a path which would help them use their resources aptly and generate output for their people.

In this race of matching with the developed nations we are leading nowhere, better we set a different goal all together. Every nation has a different potential given different kinds of resources they possess hence expecting the same output from all makes little sense. Hope the coming generation gets to learn, 'India is a developed country in the true sense'. Hence, high crime rate, such as US has high crime rate. Because it has many young people do not like to work, they depend on government assistance. Then, any kinds of low skill or low educational level job employers will feel difficult to find them to work. Then, their society will cause low skillful labour shortage challange. It is not due to US lacks enough low skill or low educational workers, it is due to they do not like to work, they feel wages are less , when their government can give any money or loss job allowance to support their lives in long time. It can enough these low educational level or low skillful level young people choose not work. Then, this US developed country will not have any young people to do any service job, e.g. driving public transport, waiter, security. When these kinds of job old people need to retire, these employers can not find any young people to replace them to do these service jobs. They can only choose to employ another old age people to replace the retired service staffs. Then, these kinds any one of service jobs can not raise their service level, their service performance will be worse or keep the same service level, it means that their performance can not perform better level to serve their clients in US society. It implies that developed country, such as US its general social service level will be worse or they can not be improved to satisfy their client needs. In this developed country's poor service environment, how to explain it can still keep its developed country's position , such as US.

However, it may bring the question -Will Developing Countries ever catch up with Developed Countries? will remain unanswered because you have rightly pointed out that leaders of developing countries have given up on the economy and they keep themselves busy with other matters. Political institutions has great impact on the development of a nation. Industrial revolution happened in England instead of any other country because England had the best political institution that time. We have been hearing that if the 20th century belonged to developed countries of North America and Europe then 21st century will be of developing countries such as India, China and Brazil. But development is the crucial word which draws boundary between two countries-developed or developing. According to the World Bank reducing poverty is the main purpose of the development. After the World War 2, many nations have had significant growth however only few have been able to catch up with developed countries in terms of per capita income. From 1940s till 1990s poor countries grew slowly, falling farther behind to rich ones in income. Only few countries such as South Korea and Singapore were able to gain rich status. Since 2000, developing nations such as India and China are economically growing and managing growth rates of above 10% per year. With such continuous growth rates, developing nations can converge with developed nations and that would mean higher standard of living and good economic and political power. But this growth is limited to few countries since many countries still have not opened their domestic market to international markets. These countries also have barriers in technology and availability and allocation of resources. So, it seems that developing countries still need more time to develop exceed to the developed countries because they, such as China, Korea, Taiwan , Singapore etc. have poor technology and shortage of allocation or resource to compare the developed countries, such as US, UK etc. even their crime rate may reduce or many young people may accept to do the low skillful or low education level service jobs in societies.

Developed countries lack effort to manufacture cheap products to sell strengths

Hence, we need to look at every economy as a company and developing a unique selling proposition becomes relevant. The United States has a USP of being the most technologically advanced and productive country. China has managed to become an exporter of cheap goods, the United Kingdom till now was a financial hub- there are chances of that changing thanks to BREXIT with the rise of Dublin. When we look at developing economies, such as India, we do not see any USP in the making. What is India's USP? I cannot think of any. People talk about demographic dividend to India in terms of a large young population. Such a population, which is largely uneducated is a demographic curse. Merely being a large market for goods and services is a bad idea for a USP. Developing countries need to introspect sometimes to look at the systemic challenges that they face. Looking towards developed economies is not always the best alternative. Such as China can choose to buy cheap product, because its technologic developement is poor. It is its strength to manufacture cheap products to sell to overseas to earn foreign income and raise GDP on export aspect. So, China may have much development chance to grow up its economy when it can decide which kinds of cheap or easier manufacturing products to sell to overseas when these countries can not supply from themselves manufactures, they need to buy from China in long time.

While the share of many western economies remained very low. However, over the years the trend started to reverse and many western countries have now become very developed while third world countries like India, China etc. continue on their journey from being developing to developed. We are currently a 2 trillion dollar economy and the eighth largest economy in the world. By 2030, India is predicted to be the fifth largest economy in the world. On purchasing power basis, India is the second largest economy in the world only behind China. Despite so many bright spots, we are faced with the paradox of being an advanced economy and still being one of the poorest in the world.

Otherwise, many such countries who are highly rich in natural resources continue to be plundered by the developed economies. Many countries continue to be haunted by the choices they made in past and turnaround being highly unlikely. They are often not helped by the injustices meted out by the developed economies who continue to take decision in their own self-interest. I feel the time has come when all the developing economies need to unite and raise their voice collectively. They need to speak about the unfair treatment meted out to them. A step in this regard has been taken by countries like India and China in important forums like UN and WTO. These breakout countries can act like role models and help create a more equitable world.

Another country is India, developing country , it may choose to manufacture and sell cheap products to any overeas countries to earn high GDP trade income. Till about 1750s, India was one of the largest economies in the world, contributing close to 25% of the world GDP. It was called the 'Golden Bird' and its products were world famed. The country has had huge trade surpluses for centuries through export of spices, finished cloth ('light woven air', it was called), and diamonds; all exotic products to that time period. It also had a thriving shipbuilding industry. There were accounts of Roman Establishments worrying about their riches syphoning off to India, because of the love of their woman towards Indian Cloth. India, thus essentially provided what the world desired & craved for, taking very few in return. This is despite the fact that it had one of the largest populations of that time. Then how come Indians achieve that richness and advancement, which seems difficult now? It is because, India was a hotbed of skilled people, who created exotic products, which were taken to the world by merchants in Indian built ships, which in turn were financed adequately by an established network of local people. So, although, India is not one high technologic development country, but it can choose what kinds of general cheap products to manufacture or catch any natural resources, e.g. growing up fishing industry, diamond industry. It is any one developed countries can not own strengths to compete to India easily.

Modern India and the ilk, are that they should spend more on Education and encourage Individual/SMEs (Small and Medium scale Enterprises), through adequate financing. The educational infrastructure should go to every nook and corner of the country like the 'temple complexes' providing accessible and affordable education, in the form of 'community colleges' in the US & 'skill enhancement centres'. Governments should support with adequate funds to create world-class universities of yesterday like 'The Nalanda', to provide cross-functional education and focus on innovation. The population should be encouraged to innovate & produce products, the world desires, like the 'light muslin cloth' or the 'iPhone' of the modern day, which shall bring huge trade surpluses. Industrialization should be decentralized through support for SMEs rather than purely going for High scale Industries. The financial infrastructure should be expanded enough to provide the financial support to every citizen, through banking services. Thus, on the whole, history can provide us with a lot of lessons on how to go about things, provided we have the interest to see from where we have come from. These lessons can be modified and applied to the current times, for we know these lands have done it before, for centuries. But, the only thing that requires here is 'Conviction' and if every country starts working on building these capacities, they becoming developed economies is just a matter of time!

Climate change will impact developed countries to continue develop

Why does climate change impact developed countries to continue develop more easily? It is one natural environment hurt problem , due to human,e.g. businessmen their damage our global natural environment behaviors, to cause any one developed countries may become developing countries in future one day in possible. I shal indicate the reasons as below:

The effects of climate change will not be uniformly distributed across the globe and there are likely to be winners and losers as the planet warms. Applying a broad brush to climate effects, developing countries are more likely to disproportionately experience the negative effects of global warming. Not only do many developing countries have naturally warmer climates than those in the developed world, they also rely more heavily on climate sensitive sectors such as agriculture, forestry and tourism. As temperatures rise further, regions such as Africa will face declining crop yields and will struggle to produce sufficient food for domestic consumption, whilst their major exports will likely fall in volume. This effect will be made worse for these regions if developed countries are able to offset the fall in agricultural output with new sources, potentially from their own domestic economies as their land becomes more suitable for growing crops. Moreover, developing countries may also be less likely to create drought resistant harvests given the lack of research funding.

Wild weather weighs on economies
The increased frequency and severity of extreme weather will weigh on government budgets. The aftermath of natural disasters often falls on authorities who are forced to spend vast amounts on clear-up operations and healthcare costs that come with experiencing extreme weather. Revenue reductions may also be experienced by countries heavily dependent on tourism or on selling fishing rights, fo

The effects on negative environment influence to developed countries and developing countries

As developed countries face an increasing strain on domestic budgets, fewer resources in the form of aid and economic development funds will flow to developing countries. The governments of these nations will be forced to channel resources away from productive and growth-enhancing projects towards countering the costs of extreme weather. Such effects will damage near-term growth prospects. Furthermore, developing countries are likely to have less capacity to rebuild. The time required to recover from natural disasters will be prolonged and if longer than the frequency in which such disasters occur, many developing economies could remain in a constant state of reconstruction.

Africa and Asia most at risk

Highly vulnerable regions in the emerging world include Sub-Saharan Africa and South and South East Asia, according to the World Bank. In South Asia, cities such as Kolkata and Mumbai will face increased flooding, warming temperatures and intense cyclones. Loss of snow melt from the Himalayas will also reduce the flow of water into the Indus Ganges and Brahmaputra basins. Meanwhile in South East Asia, Vietnam's Mekong Delta, which produces most of the rice, is especially vulnerable to rising sea levels. For Sub-Saharan Africa, food security will be a major challenge due to droughts and shifts in rainfall. Many developing nations are situated in low latitude countries and it is estimated that 80% of the damage from climate change may be concentrated. Consequently, higher agricultural yields, lower heating requirements and lower winter mortality rates are a handful of economic benefits climate change may bring, although these benefits may diminish as warming continues.

However, the prediction that developing countries will be disproportionately affected is reinforced by Standard and Poor's research on the influence climate change will have on sovereign risk. Recognising that climate change is a global mega-trend impacting sovereign risk through economic, fiscal and external performance, they find that lower-rated sovereigns appear most exposed. Based on these measures we can interpret the results in part as the susceptibility of an economy to climate change.

How poor climate change influences UK developed growth

In the UK, the average temperature is now 1°C higher that it was 100 years ago and 0.5°C higher than it was in the 1970s. As a higher latitude country, it is believed that the UK will fare better than many developing nations as global warming progresses. That is not to say the nation will escape the costs of climate change - particularly given its significant coastline where rising sea levels pose an obvious threat. According to scientists estimate of the cost of floods to the UK economy as a result of 3°C - 4°C of warming are in the region of 0.2% - 0.4% of GDP annually by the middle of the century, if flood management efforts are not strengthened.

In England, the south and parts of Yorkshire and Humberside are forecast to experience the greatest impact from flooding by 2050 . Aside from increased flooding, water availability will become progressively more constrained and droughts more frequent .Milder winters and the associated decline in cold-related mortality rates will be countered by a greater prevalence and severity of heat waves, bringing with it a higher number of heat-related mortalities. Finally, with the agricultural sector contributing approximately just 0.6% of GDP, the benefits of longer growing seasons will be marginal to the economy.

In conclusion, climate change may also indirectly affect the UK economy through global supply chains. The UK may both export to and import from climate-sensitive countries. The subsequent influence of climate change in these economies may feed through to the domestic economy through lower demand for exports or higher prices of imports.

VI

Factors Influence Human Future High Technological Development Failure

Why do developed countries need to improve on culture, education, medical technologyl development aspects?

I shall attempt to explain that why America, Japan, England and India these four countries ought need to improve on above sevearal aspects as below:

Firstly, I shall explain that why Japan still needs to improve itself country technology development, although Japan had been a technological mature development country in long time. In Japan technological development history, Japan had owned high technological development on technological products manufacture aspect, such as electronic rice cookers, artificial intelligent rice cookers cars, televisions etcl technological products. But when Germany had also began to develop high technological products in global technological prodict market. In basic, all any similar Japan technological products. Germany had also owned high technological skills to manufacture to sell in global high technological products marekt.

So, nowadays, Germany may still be Japan's high technological product main competitor. It means that global homeholders technology products consumers, car buyers must choose any Germany and Japan high technological products to compare which are better quality in order to satisfy their useful need.s Hence, in global high technological products market, Japan won't be still high technological product leader as past history. If Japan did not continue to improve its technology, Germany will be the future high technology product leader to replace Japan, hence Japan can not neglect to consider how to continue to improve its technology development.

IN the past, science and technology in Japan is focused in vehicle manufacture technology, consumer electronic, robotics, medical devices, space exploration and film industry. For example, Japan's focus on intensive mathematics education and the reverence for engineers in Japanese culture aids enginnering talent development which as produced advances in automative engines, television display technology, videogames , optical clocks etc. On aerospace exploration aspect Japan had conducted space and planetary research., aviation research and development of space and satellites. On nuclear power development technology, since 1973, Japan has been looking to become less dependent on imported fuel and start on depend on nuclear energy. On electronic development aspect, Japan is well known for its electronic industry throughout the world, and Japanese electronic products account ofr a large share in the world market. However, Japan had beed a leading nation in scientific research, particularly biomedical research.

However, all of above technology, Germany will own advance technology to replace Japan to develop its products to sell to global easily. Germany had innovated its technology, e.g. the self -driving cars of the near future depend on precise digital geolocation data to navigate to arrive at destinations. So, Germany's non-manual driving vehicles innovation may be future nay countries car users' suppliers. Also, its battery technology is also one of future high technology mission 2021. Germany government began to support the construction of autonomous capacities in battery cell production to secure technological maximally exploit the battery calue chain. Germany government should continue to support electronic battery cell manufacturers, to drive force in the growing market for electronic cars and the goals of continuing to build their motors in Germany in the future.

Is Germany technology advanced? I believe that it is true, in the index's eighth edition for 2020, Germany was named the most technologically advanced nation, followed by South Korea, and Singapore, Germany is most known for its engineering, different high technological invention etc. aspect. Why is Germany so technologically advanced? Because Germany had been an academic powerhouse for a long time and as such education is focused on technological aspect. It's education goal is for good ideas to be translated quickly into innovative products and services. Moreover, Germany also considers Hyper automation, the distributed cloud, technological development. Some technological leaders predict the future high technological development countries may include: China, South Korea, United States , Singapre , United Kingdom, Russia, Japan and Germany .

The possible number or rank technological development countries rank may be 1 South Korea rank 2 ,ay be United States, rank 3 may be Japan, rank 4 may be Sweden nowadays. However, Germany may be future rank 1 technological leader, because Germany is so good at engineering. Germany's engineers borne out of the country are world leaders in their field, reowned for their dedication to precision, function and power. Over the years, Germany engineers have maintained their reputation to help Germany technology development products to as a top exporter of machinery and industrial equipment.

Moreover, in human development history, Germany are smart, when Germans are the most intelligent people in Europe, the British have an edge over rivals in France when it comes to the grwy matter , a new league of IQ scores has shown. The scored 94 and Germans were tap of the table with an IQ of 107, according to Richard Lynn, who headed the study. However, why is German technology will be the best. The major factor for Germany's success is that it has managed to homegrown scientific research and expertise to move up the technological ladder, concentrating on innovative products and processes not easily copied or undercut by cheap wages. The textile industry is a case in point, hence it causes that future Germany's technology development may be Japan's future one main competitos in technological product development market. So, it is right time, Japan needs to continue to research its new technological invention in order to improve its technological development to be the best to compare other high technological development countries.

Secondly, I shall discuss that why US needs to improve or change itself country's culture to let many different countries people can adopt to live. For example, nowadays, COVID 19 illness is serious to influence any one country people live. IN fact, US ia a developed country, it is global countries only one leader to encourage different countries people to live. Also, US is one comfortable living people to let global immigrants to feel. But, when COVID 19 disease occurred, some US people feel that it is possible due to Chinese people , they contact COVID 19 disease to cause many US people get this kind of disease. However, it is none evidence to prove this kind of illness may be caused by Chiese to cause many US people die. So, US, opening culture began to change worse, e.g. some US people began to hate overseas immigrants to live itself country, it is possible due to many US people feel afraid to contact overseas immigrants, they may bring COVID 19 disease in their bodies, so when US people they contact these overseas COVID 19 disease immigrants, they may get this kind of disease . SO, it seems that US people's opening accept to let overseas immigrant living policy has changed to prohibit them to immigrate to live US easily.

However, I feel that US 's closing culture mind can not bring its social development to improve more easily. US ought to change its social culture has more opening cultural mind as before how it accepted different countries immigrants to choose US to live. Hence, it brings this question: What challenges US may encounter if it can be change its new cultural mind to accept more overseas immigrants to live easily? The challenges may include: American needs to understand themselves value and learn about what is important to Americans know why Americans value independence, equality and being on time. Americans will need see they are direct and informal and why competition, work ethic, and buying things are important in the US. American probably had strong traditions and culture that they valued. In the UNited States, there are also important American values are the things that are most important to Americans. For example, one of the main American values is independence. Independence is sometimes referred to US individualism. Americans are very proud of being self reliant, or being able to take care of themselves. American children tend to leave the home earlier than in oterh cultures, if they continue to live at home, they might be asked to pay rent or contribute to the house. So, Americans expect anyone who is able to work to do in order to support themselves. Also, Americans value privacy and their own space, when in some cultures wanting privacy may be seen as a bad thing, many Americans like to have alone time and may be private abour certain topic. In conversations, many Americans are private about certain things and do not want to talk about them, such as age, how much money they make, or their political, sexual and religious views. Americans often give each other more space in public situations than people in other cultures . They tend to stand with a bit of space between them, typically the distance of direct. This means that they often tell you what they think and they will be assertive about when they want.

Some peoples of American-style directness,, such as in conversation, if an American disagrees with youropinion, they might tell you, this does not mean they do not like you, just that they may have a different area. In classes, Americans may challenge their teachers' ideas. IN some culture, it is impolite to disagree with your teacher, it is never is rude to ask for help. Most Americans love to help and need very little encouragement to become good friends and neighbors.

However, I feel that America has lose equality value. Although, many newly immigrants moved to America to follow American team. They believed that if you worked hard, you could move up in society. But, today, more and more people realize the American dream is not true. Many people who work very hard do not have very much money. Often people who love from privileged backgrounds have an easier time moving up in the world. Still, the idea of equality is an important part of US culture.

So, COVID 19 disease occurrence had explained that US began have inequality culture difference causes, discrimination to overseas immigrants, e.g. Chinese. Americans discrimination behavior began to cause. American ought change itself new culture to traditional culture to accept different countires clever immigrants skills, talent people mind in order to help itself country to continue develop more advanced society to be world leader position.

Thirdly, I shall discuess why England needs to improve education. What negative impacts will happen, if UK does not continur improve education as well as its neglect on improvement education, how it will bring negative impact to its studetns minds in society? Why growth is the key to improve UK education development? Conventional wisdom states that smaller schools provide students with a better education . But studies of education systems around the world, show that growing schools could actually solve UK's poor student outcomes.

Nowadays, the UK's school system is in trouble, despite the fact that the last two decades have seen massive changes in the UK's education sector. UK education report indicated that in the past 15 years, the UK's four countries have spent $550 UK billion on operating and enhancing their secondary schools. IN the same period, England alone closed 35% of its schools (1,500 institutions) and opened almost 2,000 new ones . Nonetheless, little has improved UK education report indicated that in 2026, only 65% of all English pupils graduated with five or more grade as compared with 50% 15 years ago, at a cost od $37 billion per percentage point of improvement. The US was as a wholw spent the 8 th largest amount of 34 OECD countries, but only came, 19 th in mathemactics, 16 th in reading and 14 th in science.

So, what 's going wrong to cause UK students have worse learning performance. The reasons may include: Neglecting all four nations education reforming. Education in the UK is devolved to the four nations that make up the British union. For this reason, most of qualifications data relates only to England, although total spending figures are mostly UK wide. Academy shcools are amodel of schooling that is available only in England. There is no provision for the model in the other three nations of the UK.

The next reason is failure educational strategy. UK education report also indicated that England's strategy over the past 15 years has been to try to improve its education system by fixing its low lights , less than a third of students graduate with five or more GCE grade , reducing their projected lifetime earnings by $140,000. By putting their schools into " special measures" and offering them up for tender to other schools, it hopes that whole education system would improve. BUt, it has not . THe English have thrown more money at the proble,, spending 84% more on each child's education . Then, they did 15 years ago ($57,000 rather than $31,000), but although half their schools have improved, the other half have declined, and the overall picture is still the same. So, there are still many UK schools can not get UK government help to improve all school students individual learning effort to be better.

What would have happened if UK government had spent the last 15 years trying to grow their education system bright lights, rather than brighten , their low lights?

UK education improvement strategy is such that a similar change in strategy helped the charity save the children reduce malutrition by 80% in Vietnam over two years, after decades of getting. Instead of trying to solve the poor learning ability of student learning performing problems in their worst areas, UK educators also need to expand a similar improvement education on strategy shift in order to help transform to UK any schools reforming educational policies in success.

Hence, if England had adopted another long term countrywide educational strategy, where all schools work together to improve standards across the UK in order to access all schoools resources, facilities and entracurricular activities and it could shown that good teachers in both schools can teach anyone. Then, most of UK teachers can know their subject inside out and quickly adapt their teaching methods to different needs. Consequently, when UK can imporve most of UK students learning effort to the best performance, as better educated students are more knowledgeable, money when they can attribute their the best effort to their society in the future. Then, UK society can be developed to reach the most top level, because UK's future development must depend on its next generation's help. If future UK education can train many talent students to attribute to social different aspects, such as technology, medical , business, construction etc. different professional aspects . UK future social development may be improved to be better to compare present society development. So, UK government can not neglect how to improve all UK student individual learning performance in order to help every UK student to pursue their abilities to prepare to attribute to UK future society devleopment successfully.

Finally, I shall discuss why India will need to improve medical technology. Recently, world news reported that INdia has many people are killed by COVID 19 disease. India is the highest population country. I assume that COVID 19 disease causes many Indians die because India has no enough hospitals, clinics to provide good medical quality to serve these COVID 19 disease contact patients. Due to lack of the best medical skillful doctors and nurses. So, many COVID 19 disease patients can not be saved to their lifes, even in India society, many none of COVID 19 disease contact people, when they contact to the COVID 19 disease people, they can not give good drugs to save themselves lifes. SO, it explains why India has many people are killed by COVID 19 disease in short time . SO, it seems that India lacks enough drugs to supply to these COVID 19 disease patients to cause there are many COVID 19 disease patients die in short time.

This COVID 19 diease attracks India matter occurs, it brings these questions: IS short time shortage of drug supply factor or long time shortage of drug supply factor to cause many COVID 19 disease patients die? Can long time poor medical technology factor cause many Indians die? IS COVID 29 disease the main factor causes many Indians die? India has many people are living. So, India must eed to improve its medical technology in order to solve the number increasing of India people future health challenge. One of the most important and highly debated, elements of India society is the quality of healthcare available to patients. The use of technology increases provider capability and patient access when improving the quality of life for some India clients and saving the lives of others. The India technology role can play in improving health of India. It can help in early detection of health problems. It cn also help in data collected from tests instantly monitor, the conditon of the patient, and then relay that information to the doctors and staff of the overall healthcare system.

However, the factors have made improvement in health conditions possible in India , they may include: A downtrend in communicable diseases, a focus on prevention , reduced neonatal mortality rates, tacking antimicrobial resistance, improved nutrition, using digital health and artificial intelligence for social impact, stronger government accountability. A number of industry analysts have observed that increased accessibility of treatment is one of the most tangible ways that technology has changed healthcase. Health IT opens up may more avenues of exploration and research, which allows experts make helathcare more driven and effectve than it has ever been. Hence, future India may apply these new medical technology, e.g. virtual reality, precision medicine, health wearables, artificial organs, 3D printing, wireless brain sensors, robotic surgery, smart inhalers, they are the main treatment option for asthma and if taken correctly, will be effective for 80% of India patients.

Hence, India must need solve medical technology improvement challenge in order to keep many people lifes , in special for the talent youngers, e.g. doctors, scientists, architects, lawyers, accountants , atc. professionals. I believe that India's medical technology can not been improved to raise quality in order to save many COVID 19 disease patents their lifes. So, many of COVID 19 disease patients can not been saved by good quality if medical drugs in short time. So, if INdia does not hope to lose many young talent professionals, it must need to continue improve its medical technology as soon as possible.

How can our future social development can be improved ?

Nowadays, globalization cooperation or our societies become one society to any countries leaders is needed. I believe that countries competition will be serious, even we shall attack other countries if any one country can not accept " globalization cooperation mind". I mean that it is only globalization cooperation one way choice, then our societies can be improved or will be become better more easily.

For China and America two countries example, recently, because COVID 19 disease caused many Western and Asia countries began feel that COVID 19 disease was caused from Chinese. However, they have no evidence to indicate that COVID 19 disease must be caused from China. Although, before the year end of two years, there are some Chinese had ever travelers to US, then US had many people began to get this kind COVID 19 disease to cause many American die, when they did not believe that COVID 19 disease can cause human dies easily. Until to now, global many people had gotten this kind of illness to vause they die, when the health person contacts the owned COIVD 19 disease sick people . Although some people can be saved after they are saved by drug, but many people can not be saved, when they can not been saved by drug, even they still can not saved after they had been gotten drug. Such as US, UK, India, China, Germany , Korea, Japan, France these countries reported that they had many people could not saved to keep their lifes when they could not believe that they can get COVID 19 disease when they contact to the strange people who may owned COVID 19 diesease easily, when they are sitting down to the same table to eat in restaurants or when the COVID 19 disease strange person and the health person are talking together closely.

So, I believe that it is right time to any countries leaders need to act and to cooperate to find the method to avoid COVID 19 disease attacks any people. I mean the globalization cooperation attitude may nee to ourselves countries leaders . Our country leader can not only consider himself/herself country benefit and neglact to consider other countries benefits. If global humans hope that we can still to improve our culture to be peace or improve our space technology artificial intelligent development manufacturing to the advance level rapidly, or improve our medical technology to the best quality or improve our students learning effort or teachers teaching performance to reach the most satisfactory need to our future any one students. It is only global cooperation way to achieve global improved societies aim. If our societies or any one country leader still only consider how to protect himself/herself country businessmen benefits and leader himself/herself benefits, and rich people benefits , but they neglect to consider any one citizen benefits ,e.g. the low education, poor old age people, low income people in societies.Then, unfair and discrimination will be encouraged to occur in any one country society . Consequently when any one country low education , low income , poor old people can not feel comfortable to lieve in themselves countries. They will feel angry to complain themselves countries governments and leader individual ambitious behavior to influence these group people feel unhappy to live long time in themselves countries.

Consequently, the country's social education level will only continue to worse, even economy will continue recession, as ell as and kind of technologies won't continue improve. Due to our future any one country leader can not keep globalization cooperation mind or positive opening attitude to let any one itself country citizen feels comfortable to live forever. Then, the developed country ,e g. US, UK will not still keep technology development leading position easily. It is possible due to they only consider themselves social benefits, during this COVID 19 disease had been attacking themselves countries. So, they ought also consider other countries , they are attacked by COVID 19 disease, hoe to avoid COVID 19 disease will continue to attack any one country easily.

Hence, we only cooperate to help ourselves to find the best long time method to fight COVID 19 disease . When our countries leaders can cooperate to spend time to sit down to discuss how to fight COVID 19 disease , then I believe that our global societies may been improved more better rapidly as soon as possible in this year.

Methods to avoid future human developmend failure
Finally, I shall conclude that how we can avoid human development failure. we need to know that human is facing threat of self-benefit behavior. We can follow our development to analyze why we shall encounter failure of improvement stage in our soon future. In our past thousand years, human had developed in success from fishing, agriculture stage till to manufacture industry innovation stage, till to nowadays high technological development stage ,even our future artificial intelligent high technology (non-manual control machine stage). Although all of our past development , till to nowadays development, it seems that we can develop in success in any technological aspects

,e.g. space, computer , internet , ecommerce , medical technology etc. even future non-manual control (AI) artificial intelligent technology. But, some ways may help us to continue high technological development in success, even damage our future continue high technological development. They may include unfriend or poor culture development, lacking globalization cooperation, self -beefit mind factors.

All of above factors are any countries leades self-benefit mind or negative attitude (human behavior) to influence our future high technology continue development can succeed in possible. The reason is because that if any one country leader only considers how to protect himself/ herself country technological development beefit, it means that he/she does not allow his/her country talent scientists can discess their any new technological invention opinions to let other countries talent scientists to learn ho to improve themselves new technological invention together. This point is the main bad factor to cause human future any kinds of high technological development to delay in possible, because our any kinds of high technological development success, we must depend on global scientists can have chance to share their any kinds of new technological experiments to let they can learn why the scientist can develop the kind of product in success, or why the scientist can not develop the kind of product in success. Then, any one country scientists can absorb other countries scientists their successful or failure scientific experiements in order to improve their any kinds of new technological expeiment to achieve the most satisfactory scientific experiement demand to bring benefit to us. So, globalization cooperation is the only way to avoid human development failure absolutely.

Why do developed countries need to continue to learn how to improve new technology ?

In fact, there are different between developing and developed countries. Developing countries, such as Afria, Korea, China, Taiwan, these countries are developing, so their IT information , medical, manufacturing technology, artificial intelligence etc. different industries are not mature, they must need to continue improvement to develop their skills in order to satisfy consumers market need. Because social need had been often changing, so these developing countries scientists, businessmen need to have good learning mind to prepare to learn how technological , medical , artificial intelligent, IT knowledge in order to satisfy consumer individual new product useful need and keep market competitive effort in themselves home an overseas consumption markets both more easilu. But, why do developed countries also need to continue to learn how to improve new technology? What negative impacts will bring to developed countries their scientists and businessmen do not continue to improve their new products development or continue to research how to improve their old products to achieve the best quality to order consumers needs.

Nowadays, global consumption market competition is serious. Consumer individual need or demand is increasing, when one consumer feels the kind of old product can not satisfy his/her actual need, he/she will seek to find which brands of products, they have similar function or useful characteristics in order to make comparison to other similar kinds of products. Then, he/she will make final purchase decision. So, when the consumer had habit to use the brand of product, it does not mean that he/she will continue to use this brand of product.

He/she may be influenced to change to choose the another brand of similar function characteristics of new product to buy use in this rapid changing competitive market.

Hence, if the developed country's culture is changed to closing mind from opening mind. These developed country, such as US people can not accept to other countries people new, useful, attributing innovativ mind of ideas easily. They only consider or recognite that themselves ideas are the best or the most useful. Consequently, due to their foolish closing minds, their traditional protection themselves believes will cause difficult to continue to improve or develop, because it is possible that there are any other developed countries, e.g. UK, Germany, Japan, they have some talent people, scientists their technological skills may be proficient or more advanced to compare US, itself countries some scientists.

So, I recommend that any developed countries can not only consider to appreciate themselves countries scientists must be the most smart to compare other developed countries. Any one developed country scientists ought need to cooperate with other developed countries scientists to discuss or research any new invention together in order to help themselves technology can been improved rapidly in order invent many different kinds of new products to satisfy consumers themselves often changing useful needs in this global consumption market nowadays.

This developed country Japn is one good example to explain that why its scientists ought need to continue to improve their different technology or science skills as well as learn any new kinds of technology or science knowledge from other developed countries scientists , such as US, UK, Germany together. Because it is only one effective technology and science improvement method (way) to

Japan scientists,when they can accept the other developed scientists different new or innovated opinions as well as they can spend some time to sit down to discuss and cooperate to help themselves old products how to change or innovate new products in order to attract global consumers purchase choice. So, although, Japan had been one developed country long time, its technology development had searched mature stage in the past, But, it can not reprsent that its technology must be more advanced to compare other developed countries, such as UK, US, Germany. Because these any one developed country, their scientists still continue carry on researching how to improve themselves old products to be new. So, it seems that Japan's any old technological products, e.g. smart phones, television, washing machines, rice coolers, products won't bring more attract to persuade global consumers choices. Because US, UK, Germany etc. different developed countries scientists had began to research how to continue improve its traditional old technological products to be more attraction in order to adopt global technological products users needs. For example, developing country India, due to its medical technology is poot, if it hopes to improve itself country technology, it must need to attempt to concentrate on spending money, medical teaching resources on medical technology aspect. India's medical technology improvement must be any kinds of technologies , the most need to improve to compare IT technology, manufacturing technology, artificial intelligent technology, space technology etc. The reason is that India is the highest population country, if its medical technology's cost, it will cause many young talent people die, such as COVID 19 disease occurs to India recently. It causes many Young talent Indians die, due to it lasks enough good medical technology to supply drugs to save them. So, if India government hopes that it can have many talent high skillful technology youngers to serve itself country. It will need to consider how to improve its medical technology in order to fight any possible new kind of illness attack, instead of COVID 19 disease, when India can improve its medical technology to save many young talent scientists' lifes . Then, it won't lose many talent scientists and they can continue to attribute themselves scientific knowledge for India itself country lont time technological science development.

9 798887 047812